Women
Who Lived and Loved
North of 60

Toni Graeme

Printed in Canada

Stories compiled and edited by Toni Graeme
Digital production and cover design by Paul Lidgate, Eagle Eye Editorial
(www.EagleEyeEditorial.com)

Canadian Cataloguing in Publication Data

Main entry under title:

Women who lived and loved north of 60

ISBN 1-55212-449-5

   1. Women--Canada, Northern--Biography. 2. Canada,
Northern--Biography. I. Graeme, Toni, 1937-
FC3957.W64 2000   920.72'09719   C00-910976-5
F1090.5.W65 2000

TRAFFORD

This book was published *on-demand* **in cooperation with Trafford Publishing.**
On-demand publishing is a unique process and service of making a book available for retail sale to the public taking advantage of on-demand manufacturing and Internet marketing.
On-demand publishing includes promotions, retail sales, manufacturing, order fulfilment, accounting and collecting royalties on behalf of the author.

Suite 6E, 2333 Government St., Victoria, B.C. V8T 4P4, CANADA

Phone	250-383-6864	Toll-free	1-888-232-4444 (Canada & US)
Fax	250-383-6804	E-mail	sales@trafford.com
Web site	www.trafford.com	TRAFFORD PUBLISHING IS A DIVISION OF TRAFFORD HOLDINGS LTD.
Trafford Catalogue #00-0114		www.trafford.com/robots/00-0114.html

10   9   8   7   6   5

Introduction

Canada's North has long held a fascination for many people, most of whom never venture there but love to read about it. So, here is a collection of pieces written by women who lived North of 60. Some went up to work, or for adventure, some went with family or husbands or to catch up to their fiance or boyfriend. Some went of their own choice, others out of necessity for their husband's job transfer. Many went for short periods and then returned south; others went for short periods and stayed a long time. The experience changed every one of them. They each embraced life in the North and felt richer for the experience; even the difficulties they encountered, such as loneliness, a sense of alienation and missing their familiar culture and lifestyle, helped them mature.

Most especially these are stories from the women's perspective. They who often worked for a living as the men did but were also singly responsible for birthing and raising the family, often in his absence, and making their cabin, tent or house a hearth and home. They brought warmth to the north and gentleness to an otherwise harsh environment. They wove the social fabric of northern life, incorporating the challenges and melding the family and community so there was love and a place for everyone. Unsung heroes they are, on Canada's northern frontier.

After my own decade in the north I came back south believing it would be a wonderful experience if every young person in Canada could spend at least one year there. They would have experiences that could give them valuable lessons for the rest of their lives. One draws on and develops one's own personal resources sooner when there are no geegaws, gadgets and multitude of agencies to lean on, although the north has those for serious problems.

My thanks go to the NWT Archives office at the Prince of Wales Museum in Yellowknife, NWT for the three photos that accompany Mary Saich's story. And very many thanks to each and every woman included here who contributed her remembrances to be shared with those less fortunate!

Toni Graeme
Victoria, August 2000

About the Author . . .

Toni Graeme

Toni Graeme spent one year in Whitehorse, Yukon and nine years in Yellowknife, Northwest Territories. In both territories she traveled extensively and came to know the people and the land well. Although a passionate southern gardener, she came to love the land both within the tree line and the barrens and managed some adventuresome gardening both indoors and out as well as keeping chickens for organic eggs.

Toni's life work has often revolved around women, their needs for health and family as well as their education and in the workplace; hence her interest in collecting these short stories of women's experiences in the North from 1937 to the present.

Contents

A Yukon Bear Yarn — 1
By Marjorie (Hoggan) Bergstrand

We Loved It Then and We Love It Now — 3
By Brenda Cox

Northern Exposure — 4
By Irene Douglas

Yukon Teas — 6
By Marnie Drury

My Life and Love in Yellowknife — 8
By Lois Eskelson

What I Thought I Knew About the North — 10
By Nancy Gardiner

A Mountie's Wife Joins His Winter Patrol — 15
By Grace Gibson

Growing Up Jewish North of 60 — 17
By Leah R Glick-Stal

The Call of the North — 19
By Toni Graeme

I Went North With My Wedding Cake and Flowers in Hand — 26
By Muriel Hall

Chicken Charlie — 34
By Jean Hodgkinson

Excerpts of Letters From a Nurse in Inuvik — 37
By Mary Johnson

Magic and Mystery in the Land of the Midnight Sun — 41
By Marion Langevin

"Guess What!" — 46
By Marion Lysyk

We Went North for Five Years — and Stayed for Thirty-Two — 51
By Dolly Macara

The Black House in Dawson City, Yukon — 53
By Betty Mackie

Please See Next Page

Contents (continued . . .)

The Camp At Indin Lake   56
    By Hilda (Weichert) McIntyre

Living In A Tent On Gordon Lake   59
    By Kay Muir

A Life Full Of Hardship And Excitement   60
    By Mildred O'Callaghan

She Needed An Assumed Name To Go North   63
    By Claire Parker

The North's Legacy To Me   64
    By Helen Parker

My Experience North Of 60   66
    By Gail Pichichero

The North Has Been My 'Silver Lining'   69
    By Vicki (Cowlishaw) Pilot

Pioneering In The North   71
    By Ruth Carter Quirke

Able To Cope With Traumas   73
    By Patricia Reimer

World War II Was Young, And So Was I   75
    By Mary (Mabel Nelson) Sadler

A Christmas Letter To Mum And Dad   79
    By Mary Saich

Ice Fishing In Hudson Bay With The Inuit   82
    By Sue Shirley

A Long Time Sweetheart Brought Me To The North   91
    By Eleanor Theriault

Pets Were A No-No In Norman Wells, But . . .   97
    By Marg Wallace

A Trip On The Big Mac   99
    By Janet (Cowlishaw) Whitley

A YUKON BEAR YARN

By Marjorie (Hoggan) Bergstrand

Catherine stood, hands crossed behind her slender back as she gazed at the calm and serene surface of Kluane Lake, so peaceful and quiet. Yet she was well aware how quickly that peace could be lost in a storm riding the wind from the north, churning up the depth of the blue water, hurling sand and small pebbles onto the shore.

Staring at the high mountain ridges across the lake she thought how different these surroundings were from cities in France and Belgium where she and Ned had enjoyed the night life and easy living their lives had once provided. Though he was often away at sea on sailing ships that plied the ocean routes, she remembered their happy reunions and the excitement of his return. Their two little girls would scream with delight.

Catherine Hoggan and her children at Hootalingua on the Yukon River, about 1908

"Daddy's home, Daddy's home!" and they would dig deep into his pockets for the treasure he would bring home. The children were very dear to him as would be the six others who would later join the family in the faraway land where he went hoping to make his fortune in the Klondike Gold Rush.

But fortunes can be very elusive and while fate might favour the few, others striving just as hard could be passed over. Some, however, were blessed with the ability to find happiness in small things and make the best of whatever life had to offer. The Hoggan family were able to function in this fashion, luckily, and the children were not aware that their lives were lacking in anything. There was an abundance of love in the home, whether it was a tent by the lake in summer or a log cabin in winter.

Catherine turned back, opened the tent flaps and smiled at the four small children sleeping huddled up together. She thought of the two older girls in England; they seemed so far away and were growing up without her and their father. But being optimistic by nature she found it easy to think of the time when they would join this new northern branch of the family. Little did she know then it would be many years until this would happen.

Entering the tent she picked up the big metal bowl that was used for bread making, for the bread must be made up, kneaded and left all night to rise. The leavening agent was a hard cake of yeast that had been put to soak and soften. Though trying to move softly she had by accident hit the bowl with the mixer, known as a Sourdough spoon.

Dorothy, the eldest girl, suddenly sat up and cried, "Ma, look at the big doggies!"

Johnny, her younger brother, said "Silly, that's not a doggy, it' a grizzly bear!" Catherine turned in horror. There between the tent flaps was an enormous brown bear. With the instant reaction of a mother in defence of her young, she used the only weapon she had at hand and beat furiously on the metal basin. Dear Lord, she silently prayed, spare my children.

Her faith must have saved them, for the bear slowly backed away. She stood outside the tent hammering away as the bear ran up the beach and then into the woods. "It's all right", she called out to the children, "the bear's gone!"

Having been told that animals were afraid of fire her next move was to drag dry logs as close to the tent as she dared and to build a big fire. This she kept burning all night while standing guard over her children and hoping the weapons she held would be as effective if the bear returned. Fortunately he did not.

As she later said to Ned when he came back from his hunting trip, "My heart was in my mouth - I thought we would all be killed and eaten!"

This is Marjorie Bergstrand's re-telling of a story first told to her by her mother, about raising the young Hoggan family in the Yukon.

WE LOVED IT THEN AND WE LOVE IT NOW

By Brenda Cox

We were living in Lake Harbour on Baffin Island in January 1972. My husband was in the RCMP at the time. The detachment and house were in the same building, separated from the little settlement by a large bay. From our home, we could see nothing but northern wilderness. The settlement lights were hidden from view by large rocky hills.

One glorious night is etched in my mind as though it were yesterday. Our three children, ages one, three and five were sleeping. We had no telephone to catch up with the news on the 'other side' and it would have been a 15-minute skidoo ride across the frozen bay to hear the local news. So, this night we dressed in our warm parkas and stepped outside to view the panorama as we often did for entertainment in the evenings. There was no television or radio. It was a crisp -45. Not a whisper was heard. A feeling of peace enveloped us. Around us was a thick blanket of shimmering white snow covering the rocky hills and the bay ice. The sky was a deep royal blue, which made it seem more vivid in contrast to the snow. Directly overhead was a full moon, a perfectly round yellow ball that cast an eerie glow on the snow and ice. Over the distant hills there were the lazy northern lights floating gently as though waiting for the "Big Show" to begin. And everywhere there were stars, brilliant yellow diamonds sparkling through the white haze.

Suddenly as we watched, the sky exploded with Northern lights in a wild display of bright pink, green and red - whipping across the sky in long perpendicular and swirling motions. They were everywhere at once. We didn't know where to look. We were caught in some magic spell that took us right out of time and place. Then, with no warning, our peace was broken by the sound of many skidoos coming from behind the hills onto the bay ice below. They drove in wild disarray to become two straight lines and then they paused with their lights on. Another sound pierced the night air and we looked up to see a little plane fly over our heads and glide to a stop between the lines of skidoo headlights. As we later learned, an Inuit man was taken by skidoo to meet the plane. He had broken his leg and was being medi-vac'd to Frobisher Bay. Moments later, the plane rose quickly into the sky with its red and green lights blinking rapidly on the wings and flew into the aurora display still surrounding us. For a brief most beautiful moment it was silhouetted against the moon and then disappeared. The skidoos returned from whence they came and peace descended upon us again.

My husband and I felt all the wonderment and magic a child does on Christmas morning as we stood silently watching until the Northern lights faded as quickly as they came. Then we felt the chill of the winter night that had permeated our bodies slowly without our notice and we returned to our warm home with the feeling of having been richly blessed.

———◆———

NORTHERN EXPOSURE

By Irene Douglas

"Our company (Cominco Mines) has asked us to move." "Where?" came my reply from my comfortable Trail, BC home as I continued peeling the potatoes for supper. Rather quietly my husband said, "Yellowknife". I exploded as I dropped my knife and turned to face him, "Just say no, No, NO!"....

Have you ever watched a moving van slowly pass by your home and wind its way down your street and around the corner and up the hill carrying its cargo - all your earthly possessions and then later, sat in a strange living room, in a strange house, in a strange city, surrounded by mountains of boxes containing these same belongings? Can you catch something of the "I feel so lost" feeling?

Several months later I find myself climbing a ladder into the bowels of an old DC3 airplane winging into the Arctic along with 30 or more excited, lively Grade 6 students. The school band (consisting of bells, triangles, etc) is off to entertain Inuit school children in Coppermine, Holman Island and Cambridge Bay and I'm one of the chaperones. As we land safely on the main street of Holman Island, the whole village comes out to greet us. At each of the communities we are something like celebrities and everyone including mom, dad, grandparents, nieces, aunts, uncles, children and babies come to hear the band. The days are crisp, cold and clear, the skies are beautiful with shades of pinks, reds, mauves and blue so enchanting to this neophyte. We sleep (I use the term loosely) in sleeping bags in the schools and we all have a marvelous time with this northern adventure. I'm hardly even conscious of it, but something of the magic of the north is creeping into my bones, and I'm hooked in spite of myself. Once hooked the opportunities become unlimited.

How excited I was at my first sighting of the Willow Ptarmigan in its beautiful winter plumage, as a flock of them walked along the path in the woods just behind our house.

And even though the winter might be -40C, we would dash outside to catch a better view of the spectacular dancing 'aurora borealis' in the vivid, wispy shades of blue, green, red and gold. How we would ooh and ah!

I'll never forget walking across Frame Lake on a cold, cold night, bundled in a warm parka and sensing the stillness; hearing the crunch of the crisp snow under foot, making my way by the light of the moon and tasting deeply of the beauty and wonder of it all.

What fun to pick wild cranberries and discover no other cranberry could compare.

And the wild flowers! It became a hobby to pick and press the saxifrages, shrubby cinequefoils, twin flowers and many more and capture their beauty for hasty-notes or little pictures.

Becoming part of the church just 10 houses down the street from our home, played a significant role in our life as we entered into the lives of the people there.

But how can you top this experience? One evening I found myself sitting between the Grand Duke of Luxembourg and the Archduke of Austria at a banquet in their honour. Or, being at a dinner party where Prince Andrew at age 17 gave his first after-dinner speech. Or, imagine me all decked out in a lovely new (floor length) light blue gown complete with elbow length white gloves and dining (along with 400 others) at a banquet honouring Prince Charles who has just officially opened the new museum bearing his name. How lucky for us that we lived in the north when all the leaders of the world were curious about the north and the Mackenzie Pipe Line and N.W.T. Commissioner Stu Hodgson was delighted to entertain them which he did with a great flair and grace.

But of all these things that make the north so special to me, none is more precious than the people who came from every walk of life. The distance away from family draws one into close relationships with others, who become your family for life.

I could go on and on, but hope I've given you a flavour of how my husband, my daughter and I grew to love our taste of the north.

Then one day, five years later, came the word. "Our company has asked us to move South."

"Just say no, No, NO." But life goes on . . .

———◆———

YUKON TEAS

By Marnie Drury

My pre-impressions of the North were vague, mostly of snow and emptiness. My sister was with Canadian Pacific Airlines in Whitehorse in 1944, the year I graduated from nursing at the Royal Alexandra Hospital in Edmonton. She spoke to the local doctor about me and I received a wire offering me a job immediately. I accepted it and have been in Yukon ever since.

That first year was great fun. Many military types were still there and we had plenty of socializing. I also met a lot of the local people most of whom were very friendly.

There was lots of food, except fresh milk which I missed the most. To this day I cannot stand the taste or smell of canned milk.

The most significant person I met was my future husband, Bill. His parents were true pioneers, gracious and hospitable. The Yukon people were stimulating. Everyone was very active in various clubs and organizations. There was no such thing as 'cabin fever' then. Most people had beautiful lawns and gardens, which did not happen easily as all the soil had to be brought in.

Marnie Drury at Whitehorse, Yukon in 1944

In the fall the countryside was a riot of colour and everyone took to the bush and picked gallons of cranberries, raspberries and blueberries. The homes became redolent with the scent of jams and jellies being prepared for the long winter.

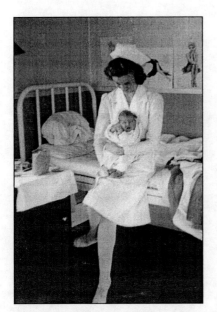

Our first house had a well but very little water. When our two children were tiny they received the first bath, then it was my turn, after which I washed the floor with the bath water! Whatever was leftover I used to flush the toilet.

In the south my idea of A Tea had been egg salad sandwiches and chocolate cake. You cannot imagine those Yukon teas! Seven or eight different kinds of sandwiches exquisitely served on Royal Derby and Doulton plates, seven or eight kinds of cakes, tarts and cookies, olives, almonds and beautiful napery. Many a young bride had relapses just thinking about giving a tea.

One of my favourite memories is of having dinner at the home of one of the 'pillars' of society. After a sumptuous repast one of the guests quietly asked to be excused in order to powder her nose. The host immediately rose, pushed aside his chair, lifted a trap door to the basement and ushered his guest down to the loo.

That's Yukon for you.

———◆———

MY LIFE AND LOVE IN YELLOWKNIFE

By Lois Eskelson

Question: Why does a young woman aged 20, one with two small children under the age of two years, allow herself to be stuffed into the last six feet of a Bristol freighter and be transported some 600 miles north of Edmonton to a settlement accessible only by air, be deposited on Latham Island in a small 'cottage' between two bootleggers - a native one and a white one?

Answer: For the love of a man of course. He chose flying as his career and wanted to help open up the North.

Question: Why would our second home be so important, the one on School Draw, a place so isolated you had to watch out for rabid wolves when you went outside to get the stove oil; the home where the 'honey bucket' froze in the winter but you were saved because you had a nice big cook stove in the kitchen and could put the bucket with its contents frozen in a heavy plastic bag in the doorway at night so it would thaw and the bag would be easy to get out of the bucket upon awakening?

Answer: My husband had a serious accident and came close to losing a leg, but thanks to the attention of Dr. Stanton happily all turned out well. The offshoot of this accident was the wonderful compassionate attention paid to us by a group of people who had been practically strangers. Every evening a couple would arrive with hot casseroles to feed the children and me. The male visitor would drive me to the hospital to visit my husband and when I returned home, the dishes were done, children bathed and ready for bed. These people became our closest friends and remain so to this day.

Question: Why was our third home like living at a 'resort', except it was no picnic?

Answer: It was Canadian Pacific Airline's old office on Back Bay. They had filled in some of the shore and about four feet of the fill protruded which left us surrounded on three sides by water while the other side was by the main ring road. Our third child was born while we were there and that meant five of us in a bedroom that had housed two huskies the previous winter! And what a mess! It seems the keepers of the huskies found it easier to just throw more straw in the dogs room rather than ever clean anything of it out. To add to my work load, I now had diapers to wash - and only one 45 gallon drum of water available per week. Even so, after the isolation on School Draw I enjoyed all the activity around us now. We lived within 30 feet of Wardair's dock, with planes forever coming and going with freight and passengers. Mind you, I could have lived without some of the added attractions seen through my kitchen window, like some of the men who needed to relieve themselves after being confined on a long flight without toilet amenities!

Question: Why was our fourth and last lodging above the seaplane base in Old Town not a step up? After all, it did have running water.

Answer: Living at the job site meant that even when you were not on the job it was on you. People were there, sober or drunk, all hours of the day and night. Our fourth child had arrived and although I loved the place, and the people, and a party - I found it just too difficult trying to raise a young family in the 'party atmosphere' that took over all else in a booming Gold Town.

Highlights of the year, besides Christmas, included trips 'out' (south) just before winter freeze up and spring break up. More than a dozen trips on bush aircraft with enough exciting experiences to make a book in themselves. The journey took at least two days, sometimes sitting on the floor of the aircraft, legs outstretched with one or more of the four children who were under the age of six sitting on top of them. When the destination was reached I was dragged on my bottom to the doorway where it was necessary for extensive massage in order for my legs to come back to life so I could stand on them!

I was a member of the D.M.S. (Daughters of the Midnight Sun), president in 1956 and helped produce their first cookbook. Twice a year on the longest and shortest days of the year we left Daddies and babies at home and let our hair down, many a good friend was made and we had a ton of fun and laughs. Those gals were a super group.

Question: Why would I choose to do it again?

Answer: For a hundred reasons and best of all:

1. We helped open up the North and I believe that we are stronger and better people because of it.
2. It's beautiful country and two of our sons were born there.
3. We made very close friends there who are still near and dear to our hearts.
4. Most importantly, I'm still with and 'love that man of mine'. We went on to have seven children, sixteen grandchildren and five great grandchildren — to date.

Therein lies the final answer.

——◆——

WHAT I THOUGHT I KNEW ABOUT THE NORTH

By Nancy Gardiner

I took the call in the boardroom of the Sun Life Building in downtown Toronto. I was hired! I was going to Yellowknife to work for a weekly newspaper - News North. That gave me a week to pack my belongings and sell my furniture from my bachelor apartment.

People trooped into my apartment to buy my TV and guitar as the packers were taking out the remaining boxes. The guitar went for five bucks, my TV for ten dollars. Someone got lucky on my move. I hoped I would too.

All I new about the North was what I had learned in school. And that was nothing. I knew more about gold mines in Africa than I did about the North or its people.

I had many misconceptions. I thought I'd find polar bears near Yellowknife. Sachs Harbour in the Eastern Arctic would have been more likely. People told me to sell my fan. I could have used it in the mid-70's summer temperatures.

Some Southerners have always wanted to come north. Since I didn't know much about it, I looked at it as an adventure. But I hadn't always dreamt about coming North.

I learned there was a single road out of Yellowknife. Actually it was a highway. My best friend Lynne joked that bank thieves never made it out of town because the RCMP just put up a roadblock. Either that or they waited at the airport.

All joking aside, Yellowknife did seem extremely remote. I pictured Lynne in a bleak room with stark white walls in a bleak climate. I pictured a bare light bulb hanging from the ceiling. There was no warmth. But I was missing part of the puzzle.

MY ROOTS

I was born in Montreal and moved to Ottawa when I was 11 years old., the daughter of an RCMP Chief Superintendent with the Security Service. I was taught at an early age not to tell anyone my business.

I grew up in an atmosphere of thick cigar smoke and basement poker games on an RCMP blanket. Cocktail parties and adults engaged in secret meetings were not unusual occurrences. My parents had met the Queen. My father had guarded various foreign leaders and royalty on state visits. He spoke about Canadian prime ministers as if they were his ultimate bosses.

It wasn't until I was older that I realized not everyone was friends with the FBI, CIA,

M15 and foreign diplomats. It was not unusual for my Dad to be away for extended periods and we weren't really sure where he was. Someone would drive up in an un-marked car and take him away. He still can't tell us where he went.

My Mom was Italian and Irish. She had a firecracker temper which I have probably inherited to some degree. She was one of six children in the Marzitelli clan. Her father built up Verona Construction, as my Aunt Connie says "from nothing".

We were third generation Canadians. My granddad lived in Montreal across from the Belmont Park fairgrounds. We were a close Italian family, where three sisters, a brother and my granddad all lived on the same street. Sometimes we went to granddad's for lunch. That usually meant "Pastavazoooooo!"

My cousin and I were the first to go to the University of Ottawa. I then took a two-year journalism course at Algonquin College. That's where I met Lynne who later worked in private radio news in Yellowknife. She was the one who told me there was a job opening in Yellowknife.

MOVING NORTH

The drive to the Toronto Airport took at least half an hour. The drive from Yellowknife airport to downtown took maybe 10 minutes.

I was met at the airport by my friend Lynne, my new editor and their respective boyfriends. The first thing that struck me were the huge wolf-skin gloves on idiot strings worn by my editor. No anti-trapping fur people here, I thought to myself. The second thing that struck me was the size of the huge ravens. No birds of prey bigger than a raven, I thought to myself.

We piled into a pick-up truck and had a five-minute tour of Yellowknife. There were two grocery stores and a handful of restaurants. You could walk just about anywhere in town. We stopped at the office where my luggage strap snapped in the cold.

Nancy in Yellowknife. Photo by Lynne Boyer

It was February 5, 1985 and 40 below zero. I thought I was at the end of the world. Nothing had prepared me for this. I had never experienced that kind of weather until I came north. There is a dryness with 40 below that makes the skin on your face cringe. It is easy to lose pedestrians in clouds of ice fog in the freezing temperatures.

I had originally been hired by News North to go to Inuvik, where the Mackenzie River empties into the Beaufort Sea. But the owner Jack Sigvaldson (Sig) assigned me to the Yellowknife office to be trained. I ended up staying there a year.

My first assignment was to cover David Crombie's visit. He was then the Minister of Indian and Northern Affairs. Among my other assignments were to cover the aboriginal organizations such as the Assembly of First Nations, Dene Nation and forums discussing division of the N.W.T.

NORMAN WELLS

During my time with News North, I traveled to most of the communities in the South Slave, Sahtu and Deh Cho areas. Travel was largely by Twin Otter aircraft and Islanders. I was once assigned to cover the opening of the Esso pipeline facility at Norman Wells. National reporters had flown in for the big event. David Crombie and the N.W.T. leader at the time, Richard Nerysoo, were in attendance.

Esso had put on a big spread of Arctic Char for the visitors. There must have been 300 people at the ceremonies. Those were the days when oil money seemed as endless as the eternal flame.

Afterwards reporters went inside the media trailers to file their stories back home. There were two phones; one was a regular phone, being monopolozed by a 'southern' national paper reporter. The other phone was a pay phone. About 15 reporters were lined up to use it. We all joked about ways to make the line shorter quicker. Like telling people in front of us there was a breaking story happening in the buffet. Or telling the southern reporter the pay phone was for him and making him stand in line.

We later boarded an Islander aircraft. The propellers are right beside the passenger windows. When they start up the plane rattles, hums, spits and twitches. The pilot kindly suggested we plug our ears. I was amazed when five adults obeyed and did indeed plug their ears on take-off. We all looked like a bunch of kids waiting for a balloon to pop.

ON TO AKLAVIK

One assignment took me to Aklavik to cover bravery awards. The Commissioner of the N.W.T., John Parker, presented them. His gracious wife, Helen, was there too.

I expected plaques and medals would be handed out. One thing I have learned living in the North is to not ever expect anything to be a certain way. You'll be surprised. And was I ever surprised when the community people behind the stage curtain hauled out an outboard motor for the presentation. The 'Kicker' as it is called locally, had a huge bow on it. When I thought about it, it made sense. It was practical and something the person could use. It gave a new meaning to award presentations and I have never thought of them the same way since.

After the awards ceremony, we flew back to Inuvik in a twin-engine airplane. I was seated directly in front of the Commissioner and his wife. The plane wasn't in the air five minutes when I heard a thud and a piercing scream. I looked into the aisle and there was Helen sprawled on the floor. Seems her canvas seat hadn't been installed properly. So on take-off she was sent flying. Lucky she had a sense of humour.

FORT FRANKLIN (Deline)

Once I was sent to cover the Dene National Assembly in Fort Franklin. The one hotel in town was a large trailer. The 'other' hotel was the RCMP jail. I knew the hotel was full and didn't want to stay confined for a week, so I brought along a tent. I also brought along my portable laptop, sleeping bag and suitcase for my trip to Calgary at the end of the assembly. I was met at the airstrip by a three-wheeler ATV (all terrain vehicle) hauling a tiny luggage trailer. I was able to pile all my luggage on it. Otherwise I would have had to walk as there were no cabs. There was also no bus. This was it. Since it was a "dry" community, we were advised not to bring any liquor. I gladly obliged.

Even though I thought the hotel was full, I went over to see if someone had canceled. Yes, indeed. There was room for one person and I was that lucky person. So for $125 per night (meals included) per person, I was able to share two bunk beds with three strangers.

I had the upper bunk. The first night I awoke unexpectedly. I saw an arm coming through the window. It was going toward the TV right bedside the window. I yelled: "Hey, what are you doing?" in my sternest and most startled voice. The arm retracted and disappeared.

I flew down the bunk ladder without hitting any of the rungs. By now, my roommates were awake. We never did see the arm again.

While in Franklin, I filed my stories by telex since I didn't know of anywhere in town with a phone jack to plug in my modem.

That meant going over to a stranger's house and borrowing her telex. That stranger ended up becoming a friend the more I visited. Helena even taught me how to make homemade bread. I pounded out my stories on tape and sent them at night while she pounded out the dough. The whole time the sweet scent of bread was wafting into my stories.

OUT OF TOWN

There were some communities where the entire population appeared to be 'out of town'. One was Colville Lake. When I arrived on the airstrip (there was no airport), the bush pilot went to his fuel cache and the rest of us walked into town. Everyone was out hunting. In a community of less than a hundred people it was easy to understand there was only one person left in town. His job was to turn out the lights, that was lucky for us. We had lunch at his place.

Another absentee community I visited was Aklavik. It felt like everyone was out of town when I put my truck into the ditch outside The Bay (now Northern Stores). I was trying to follow skidoo tracks into what I believed was the parking lot.

When I searched the town, no one was around. I finally found some out-of-town construction workers inside a nearby building. They laughed when I told them what happened. I asked if they had a pick-up truck. They looked at each other and laughed but didn't answer me. They agreed to help out though. They said, "Meet at the truck".

I thought it a little odd, so I waited at my 45-degree angle truck in the ditch. Along came this really tall loader. No problem getting the truck out. They told me that everyone in town was at a funeral.

JEAN MARIE RIVER

I'll never forget Jean Marie River, a placid town of about 50 people. Our pilot taxied his small twin-engine plane right into town. It's a weird sensation driving past a kid's school in an airplane. We were there for the opening of a nursing station. Bruce McLaughlin was the Minister of Health at the time. He was there too.

Barb, a CBC reporter, and I hadn't eaten all day. Being new to the North, I expected to eat in the community. I expected a restaurant. I have learned not to expect anything anymore. There was no restaurant. The snack bar was closed. We were starving. We were there all day with no food and feeling mighty silly.

After the nursing station opened, the local Community Health Worker served up some crackers, cheese and canned ham. Barb and I ate all the meat in sight.

We looked at each other and I said, "I hate canned meat." But it sure tasted good that day.

———◆———

A MOUNTIE'S WIFE JOINS HIS WINTER PATROL

By Grace Gibson

In 1957 Port Harrison was a small community of several Eskimo families who worked for the white run establishments such as the school, nursing station, church mission and radio station. It was also a one-man RCMP detachment (my husband Ross Gibson being in charge at the time). I was often left alone to do those duties when Ross went on patrol. But I also frequently went along when Ross went in the 'Peter head' to check the outlying camps.

Winter came very early in November. By April I had persuaded Ross to take me on a patrol 150 miles north. Father Steinman at Povungnituk (Pov) had an outbreak of the 'flu and needed medical supplies.

On April 15th, 1958 at 7 am we left Port Harrison for Pov. I was well dressed for the trip with long johns, slacks and sweater, down filled parka and pants, and over this, a caribou parka. On my feet were heavy socks, skin boots and over these a second pair of caribou skin boots.

There were two dog teams of ten dogs each. Ross and Willia, an Eskimo Special were on one sled team and Laucassie and I were on the other.

The day was nice and warm, about -10C. The dogs ran beautifully. Four hours later the temperature stared to drop and it began to snow. Every 4-6 hours we stopped to rest to dogs, have tea, soup and bannock and a "comfort" break for me. It was no easy task considering the layers of clothing I had on.

By late afternoon a real blizzard was blowing. We met an Eskimo family returning from trading at Port Harrison and went to their camp for the night. Willia built an igloo and put a tent over the top of it. Skins, food boxes, etc. were put inside and we settled down for supper and the night. I was pushed through the opening after removing my parka and boots. Supper was dehydrated chicken stew and tea and bannock.

Around 9 pm we prepared for bed. A caribou skin was laid fur side down, then another skin with the fur side up, then our grey RCMP blanket, on top of this we put our parka's, pants, boots and mittens. Then the sleeping bags were snapped together to form a top blanket. At this point we put out the prima stove and crawled into 'bed' - fully clothed.

The storm increased and the temperature fell to -25C and by midnight the tent on top of our the igloo came loose and Willia had to go out and tie it down again to the oil cans. I spent most of the night reaching out to check the snow blocks. The next day was spent in the igloo playing cards, eating and drinking tea. That night the storm ended and we

15

were able to continue our journey. It was a bright sunny day, the snow was heavy and the dogs were slow, the usual routine. I went to sleep and fell off the sled!

The fourth night we were about 80 miles from Pov. The dogs were tired, we were tired and sunburned and Ross's fingers were frostbitten from helping me out of my wind pants a few times a day. I am sure he was making himself a silent promise to never take me on a winter patrol again.

The next afternoon Pov was a welcome sight. Father Steinman had five babies ill in the mission and one in the kitchen. The much-needed supplies had been delivered. We enjoyed a couple of days rest and returned to Port Harrison.

The trip home took only three days and five other teams accompanied us. What a sight we made — seven teams with 6-10 dogs per team racing down the river to see who could reach the Hudson Bay Store the first.

At last I was home from my first, and last, winter patrol.

————◆————

GROWING UP JEWISH NORTH OF 60

By Leah R Glick-Stal

I was conceived in Yellowknife, born in Winnipeg and raised in Yellowknife. I went through the public school system in Yellowknife. After completing my BA at the University of Toronto, I moved to Tel Aviv, Israel where I worked for the Australian Embassy. After I married, my (now ex-) Israeli husband and I moved back to Yellowknife, where we lived for two years and had a son. I left Yellowknife for the last time in 1988, for Edmonton where I went back to college and graduated with an Honours Degree from Northern Alberta Institute of Technology. From there I sojourned for a time in Westbank, BC to be with my parents when my marriage failed, and finally, to Victoria, where I now work for the Ministry of Transportation and Highways. A lot of traveling for an ex-Yellowknifer!

What do I recall about Yellowknife? The asthma attacks when the temperature dropped below minus 25C. The first time I saw a black person in the flesh. The way the northern lights seem to move whenever you whistled at them. Caribou Carnival as a child and the toilet paper rolls from heaven! The freedom to go out with friends or play outside (unsupervised) and not have to worry that someone was going to attack you. I remember Miss Mill's math class at Sir John Franklin School and still think of her whenever I use my calculator! and my grades 4 and 5 teacher, Miss Gordon. If anyone has her address - I would truly love to get in touch with her as she left a mark that propelled me through university and college. Working at my parent's store - Yellowknife Radio and having my best friend, Brenda Sian who lived in the 'boonies' at Con mine.

The hardest part? Growing up as one of the handful of Jewish families in a community isolated from the mainstream of Judaism. Always being on the "outside" is hard. We were always different. There were times when I just felt that I didn't belong.

Who do I admire the most? My parents for having brought us up with the attitude that all people are equal and that all beliefs had a place in the world. My parents came to Yellowknife in the 40's and were considered what I would call, one of the pioneers. My Mom came up for a few years and stayed 34! and my Dad was there for 40 years.

My parents taught us many of the Jewish traditions that they had learned while growing up. My father tried to teach us Hebrew so that we could follow the prayer services. My Mother kept a kosher home so that we could learn the dietary rules of our ancestors. They instilled in all of us, a pride of being fortunate to live in Canada where we could openly practice our religion and still be safe.

Of course, as a youngster, I didn't appreciate these lessons although my non Jewish friends were most envious that I did not have to go to school on either the major Christian or the Jewish holidays. What traditions or religious rules my parents didn't know, I learned while at University and then later when I lived in Israel.

While I suffered only a few anti-Semitic comments, each one drove a knife into my heart. I wondered why they picked on my religion, when I had not attacked theirs.

I remember fondly that one of my closest friends, Diane (nee Johnson) Thursby's birthday always fell during the Jewish festival of 'Passover'. During this period there are restrictions on what kind of food we are allowed to eat - and you guessed it - birthday cake from flour, was not one of them. Every year her Mother would take the PASSOVER cake mixes (made from potato starch) and other permitted foods and use them as part of the regular birthday party so I could join in. I have never met another person who would go to so much trouble so that one child could attend the party.

Growing up Jewish in the north, meant that there were few young Jewish men around (other than my brothers), so dating was a difficult and restricted pastime.

Can you imagine explaining the North to people in Israel? The tourism office in Yellowknife shipped a package of maps, booklets and stickers over to me in Israel, and I became the unofficial ambassador for the North! People in the Middle East just couldn't believe there were Jews living in such a cold place.

As the longest standing Jewish family in the North, Jewish visitors were given my parent's address and phone number. Many visitors from around the world visited our home. In a large city we would not have had such an opportunity to expand our horizons.

I made several solid friendships in Yellowknife; friendships that I don't think would have developed so strongly in the south. Circumstances were just so different in Yellowknife. When you made a friend, you made a friend for life.

———◆———

THE CALL OF THE NORTH

By Toni Graeme

It was a long, hot and dusty drive along the Alaska Highway. My only car problem had been a flat tire 5 miles outside of Vancouver on the freeway! I'd left Vancouver five days earlier for a new adventure in my life and now I was finally here, Whitehorse, August 1978. But I felt a sense of disappointment as I drove the last couple of blocks towards the city's main intersection. Not the weather, for it was great, and not the look of things around me for it seemed clean, what then? My expectations perhaps? 'Well, I'm here anyway" I said to myself, "so just calm down, settle in and get to know the place".

Back in 1947 my mother had taken my brother Jon, sister Sue and I up on a Princess boat, then onto the White Pass train from Skagway to Whitehorse and from there on to Dawson City on one of the famous paddle wheelers which is now 'beached' for tourists to explore on land. The memories that stand out most are of the paddle wheeler clinging to the shore at many points along the river, while men ashore threw logs (well chucks of trees, actually) into the belly of the boat so we could ply many more miles to the next boat-belly-filling source of fire and energy to get us to Dawson City.

A paddlewheeler permanently berthed in Whitehorse for tourists to view, 1979

And then there was the cook who would give us each an orange and make happy faces with icing for the eyes and mouth, we went through a lot more icing than oranges because he would give us refills! Even though a child I appreciated the soft summer skies and breezes and to walk along the railway tracks at Carcross and smell the chamomile growing wild while we stopped to unload freight, and, days later in Dawson City, attending an Anglican church service in the tiniest church I had ever seen and staying for their tea afterwards. And having to drink powdered milk, the only milk available in the North then, it was my absolute horror drink and I would plead a stomachache or 'I'm too full' to avoid it.

Now fast forward to 1978, my first stop after the drive was a bar for a nice cold beer. The T and M, right in the centre of town had a gold prospector atmosphere. There were several huge eggs, maybe geese? coloured gold, each mounted on a little box and set behind glass in the wall. There were two tables of men sitting around drinking and talking about mines and creeks - looking for all the world as if they had just come in from sluicing operations on their claim in a creek somewhere in the bush. This, 90 years after the big rush. Bars are plentiful; in Whitehorse in 1978 there were 43 in a population of only 10,000!

Speaking of prospectors reminds me of a one-day drive I took into the bush. I stopped at a pretty creek and got out and had a picnic lunch then wandered up and down the creek imagining what gold panning would have been like when suddenly, I heard a click and an angry voice yelling at me. I turned around to see a short raggedly dressed fellow with a rifle up on his shoulder yelling hysterically, I guess he thought I was a claim jumper, but I tell you I did not wait to make out what he was yelling so I moved...and fast!

I settled into Whitehorse for a year, staying at the 'Y' where they had cluster-apartments, usually four bedrooms with a kitchen and living room. I had a single room but others were double rooms. A couple of the girls were from small Yukon settlements working in Whitehorse and another couple were, like myself, here for the experience and adventure.

I had a variety of jobs there, one month in a Woolworth's store where the floor staff were all women and the manager was a man. I became a bit provocative at the weekly staff meetings asking about company policies regarding overtime and pay rates and could a woman get promoted, etc. The manager bore it, knowing, I am sure, I would give up and quit in due course. I was started off in the toy department because, I was told, "you have several children so you will be an expert on them!" Two weeks later, I was advised I was transferred to women's wear because I was the best-dressed female staff member! I found Woolworth's to be far too paternalistic for my comfort so I left that job. Next I was part-time resource person for the Status of Women and loved it immensely. The Yukon women were fantastic and the work rewarding, assisting their efforts to improve family legislation, helping local women open a Transition House for Women, primarily battered women at the time, and initiating a Celebrity Auction which was a good money raiser (and I hear still is) for the Status of Women but also a delightful free fun evening, well free if you did not bid and win a celebrity! We put it on during Sourdough Days, a winter festival to help one and all get over the cabin fever that can grip northerners in February and March due to the long dark winters.

Having a car meant I could get about easily, so I revisited Dawson City which is a shadow of its old self; Faro, a mining town where I had a native woman friend (who ended up buying my car when I went on to Yellowknife); Carcross, where I had walked the railway tracks 31 years earlier; and also I visited a general store from long ago. Overall not much seemed to have changed there.

On a drive to Haines Junction in Yukon one weekend I stopped at a graveyard and found many pilots' graves and those of people who had had a connection with flying in Yukon. I have discovered this a great way to learn about local history.

A friend from the 'Y' and I went to Juneau for a weekend and enjoyed memories of the gold rush of '98 from their perspective, really not too different from Whitehorse. Everywhere lots of bars (in 1978 in Whitehorse there were 43! for a population of 10,000) and little gold rush/olden days boutiques selling variations of gold nuggets and assorted jewelry featuring nuggets real or pretending depending on how much you wanted to spend; lots of black coral jewelry, always the black and white photo of the climbers up the snowy Chilkoot Pass; key chains with tiny mukluks on them, and the little mukluks alone which are often used as a pull cord on zippers of parkas; and cookbooks featuring Sourdough Bread and wild meat recipes. We also visited a beautiful glacier for a day. A fellow I met there gave me his treasured Sourdough Bread recipe.

By March of '79 I felt restless. I was not ready to come back to the south so took out a map, looked north, well, that looked a little too bleak for this tree lover! I looked eastwards and there was Yellowknife. The only connection I'd ever had was having known a girl at boarding school whose father was a doctor there. Yellowknife is not famous for it's highway system so I sold my car and that financed my one-way airline ticket.

I loved Yellowknife from the minute I got off the plane and walked across the tarmac to the airport building. The Friday I arrived was the weekend of Caribou Carnival, their version of Sourdough Days in Whitehorse. I booked a room at the 'Y' for two weeks till I got my bearings and spent the weekend watching Inuit sport games, admiring the physical feats of the Strong Northern Man and Woman competition; among many physical challenges they carry heavy sacks (In Whitehorse it is flour); do igloo building - there is enough packed snow on the ground in Yellowknife by then to cut out the blocks they need to make an igloo and enjoying many entertainers that abound. There are many games they make into competitions too and Dene, Inuit and 'others' all compete.

In my first job, doing clerical work, with the federal government department that supervised drilling operations in the oil and gas and mining fields I met a woman who, with her husband, had bought a lodge where Graham and Duncan Lakes join. They invited me to fly up in their small plane with their family for a long weekend. So with my Scottish adventuring spirit it wasn't likely I'd pass up an invitation like that. One of the Conservation Engineers was also going up, but on a charter with his family, another couple and their children. They were camping out about 200 yards from my friends lodge.

It was summer and definitely mosquito time so we were well doped up with Muskol. Within a few hours of our arrival we caught some fish and started to cook supper. The kitchen had only a screen, no window so the aroma of the cooking could waft about the area. Soon one of our party spotted a black bear coming along the opposite shore about 300 yards away. He was heading towards the remnants of a little bridge that crossed some small rapids that ran between the two lakes and towards his supper I guess he thought. The alarm was sounded! We had no guns so what were we to do? My friend turned the stove off albeit somewhat after the fact! The men from the nearby camping group joined the men in our group, they stood on the bank and yelled at the bear to 'Go away', 'Shoo', 'Get lost' and so on. My aim was to get photos of the whole show so I dashed up to my room to discover I had locked my door with the camera inside and I had no key, drat! and my friend informed there was no way at this point she was going to hunt for a key to anyone's room...dealing with the bear was priority number one. Double drat!! For whatever reason after about 20 minutes the bear decided to forsake this crazy lot of yelling and arm waving humans and he moved off down the lake way from us. After that we had a tame weekend, eating and fishing and admiring the beautiful scenery and sunsets. It was a great respite from work in the office.

Six months later I moved to a job with Canada Employment where, as a counselor, I traveled a great deal (10 days to two weeks every month) for four years in the Indian communities and Inuit settlements counseling on education and training relevant to the potential for available work. I was once on a two-seater charter plane returning from a day of interviews in Rae Lakes. Our plane, with no instruments, was required to be back in Yellowknife before dusk, which at this time was 4 p.m. The flight should have taken an hour but after 45 minutes when I could see no sign of the lights of the city I asked the pilot where we were. He didn't know and shrugged. Are we lost, I asked? He shrugged again. I felt panicky but refused to act up. I asked for his map and spent five minutes searching the land below looking for distinctive outlines of lakes, (you can usually see a dark line around them as the banks along the shoreline are not covered with snow) and then find it on the map. Finally I spotted one, I pointed it out to the pilot, he grinned, shrugged and changed course by a few degrees. We actually landed 10 minutes past the deadline time. These small planes did not have instruments for landing hence the requirement to take off and land only in daylight. It took a while for the knot in my stomach to relax.

I had made the trip from Yellowknife-Cambridge Bay and return many times and on the last trip I made I sensed about 8:45 pm we should be commencing a descent into Yellowknife - but we weren't. I waited five minutes then asked the stewardess to ask the pilot when we would be in YK (as they call it for short). She came back and said :Oh, shortly". So I waited again. A second time, now about 9:15 pm I asked her and suggested we must be lost. She went up and didn't come back. Shortly afterwards we banked to the right and then we banked to the left. She whispered to me as I was leaving the aircraft that they had lost touch with the beacon signal they use to find their destination airport! They had been lost! I concluded either they had fallen asleep late in the flight (and no wonder some would as they can have terrifically long days and challenging flying conditions) or maybe they had a card game going- oh just kidding NWT Air pilots! I just knew intuitively after so many flights when we ought to be arriving. But all ended well. I'm sure many a northern pilot would scoff at my story but it's my story and I'm sticking to it!

Food on airlines in the north in the '80s consisted of a bunwich with meat or cheese and butter and coffee. And believe me you wanted to be on the early leg of the flight to get both fresh! A flight path could be Yellowknife-Cambridge Bay-Spence Bay-Cambridge Bay and back to Yellowknife in one day. Leaving Yellowknife very early am and returning around 10 pm. Needless to say the remaining bunwiches and coffee were none too fresh on the trip home. The noise of the DC6's was terrific and just before I left the NWT in '88, I was diagnosed with some hearing loss, likely from so many noisy flights. One often had to really raise your voice to have a conversation with a seatmate. But it was surprising how I mastered sleeping for an hour or longer in spite of it.

I noticed that there was not much in the way of survival supplies on board most flights so I asked my office if the Unemployment Insurance Investigator of the day, Jim Grady, an ex army fellow who had experienced survival exercises with the army in the Arctic, could lead a course for us to learn about surviving in both summer and winter. The cold and lack of food sources were more of a survival concern than the crash itself. I felt a lot more reassured after that course. It became a very successful and valuable experience for many people after Grady enlisted an ex army pal, Jim Peterson, to help him develop the course they delivered on a fairly frequent basis.

The friend and I who shared a place with at Prelude Lake bred Samoyed dogs, a hardy breed and most affectionate. They are easy to train with just a cross look and voice so there is no need to hit them. Nina, so petite, and Yuri, big boned and broad shouldered, were a great pair together until one morning three or four wolves who had been attacking dogs around the lake cornered Nina and she met her animal-Maker in doggie heaven. As with so many pets, she had such an appealing personality it was like losing a close family member.

Nina and Yuri, bred in Yellowknife in 1984

I took up cross country skiing in Yellowknife and loved the quiet environment, swishing through the trails or across an open lake, it's a comforting sound, so gentle and easy going and when you stop you can't hear a thing except perhaps the odd cracking of ice or a lump of snow that falls off a tree branch. It is so delightful with the sun so bright and the sky so blue and the air so clean you feel sad that everyone in the world can't experience this. I've often thought it would be wonderful if every Canadian had a chance to spend a year in our north country.

Another quiet experience I had was when visiting a community in the Central Arctic and I went for a 'walk' out onto the tundra one afternoon. I went out about a mile and a half and suddenly felt a moment of fear, what if I lost the community? I turned around and could just catch sight of the school which was a bright orange colour so decided I'd probably gone far enough unless I wanted to disappear! I sat down on a rock and listened to the silence for about half an hour. It's a thoughtful experience, a wonderful chance to just be, to be so alone and no one to interrupt you, but a bit scary in another way in that you realize you aren't comfortable after a bit without people and you get an urge to rush back to them. I wonder if hermits experience this too but have more fortitude to stay on by themselves. For myself I went back to the community much refreshed.

How delightful it was to have the CBC everywhere I went in the North, places that were up to 3,000 or 4,000 miles apart but always the familiar voices, programs like Peter Gwosky, Cross Country Checkup, Gilmour's Albums and so many more, even the 10 a.m. time check!

I moved south in March of 1988, went back in the fall of 1988 to live for two months and manage the NDP federal election campaign in the Eastern and Central and High Arctic, which is called Nunavut today. It is like no other campaign work experience in the country! There are of course no lawn signs (we stapled them to buildings) as it is Precambrian Shield territory and only rocky. The largest community was Iqaluit with about 3,000 hardy souls, 1/3 Francophone, 1/3 Inuit and 1/3 'other' so all literature had to be printed in three languages, Inuktutut, French and English and much of the Inuktutut literature had to be in Orthography and syllabics as the Inuit in the west use the former and in the east they use the latter. CBC made time available on the radio for the candidates and in each community there was a certain time every day for community announcements and they too gave the candidates time as they were not able physically or financially to get to every one of about 60 settlements.

All of my seven daughters visited or stayed to live awhile. My youngest daughter, Karen married there, a young Metis boy, Wayne Mercredi, whom I couldn't have been fonder of if he was my own son. I was saddened it did not work out for them but she remarried and had her first child there. My eldest daughter, Janet, came up from Toronto, in the summer of 1983 to do a boating trip down the McKenzie River with my brother, myself and a friend, ah but that's another story, she tells it later in this book. Pamela came and stayed for a summer but being pregnant decided to go back to Vancouver to have her baby and settle there.

Sally came for a long weekend and went swimming when we visited friends Lowell Ann and Peter Fuglsang at their cabin on River Lake.

Vicki came and stayed four years, married young Bob Pilot, born in the North, who then joined the RCMP, and after a six-year stint in BC with the force they are now back in the North two years in Baker Lake, two more years in Fort Smith and now, in 2000, Iqaluit.

Lisa, Pamela and Karen at Prelude Lake, NWT in 1983

Yvonne came to visit with her baby Jessica; Lisa came up with Naomi, boyfriend George came a bit later, they had another daughter Tonya Jean before returning to BC.

I've met ex Northerners almost everywhere I've traveled, in India, Africa, Portugal, Asia, Singapore, Thailand, Yucatan, Belize and across Canada. It feels like a little visit back to the North when we reminisce together. I have been back twice for visits and will go again.

Perhaps by the time I do go again many of my friends will have ended up in the south but I'll go anyway, for the wonderful skies - anytime of year they are so incredible. In the clear crisp winter the stars are so incredibly bright you can see them twinkling and even see their colours; the Northern Lights start their jumping or streaming across the sky when you least expect it and it feels like something between a miracle and magic, the movement, colour and breadth leave you awestruck.

I would put on my down-filled skidoo suit and lay on the snow to observe them, (one night I even saw a meteor) standing you could get a stiff neck looking from side to side as though watching a tennis match. In the summer the sky is a lovely soft clean clear blue and the sunsets are absolutely gorgeous. There are a variety of reds and one I saw many times which I called raspberry colour - it was my all time favourite, the reds meld into bright deep oranges, then down to peach and yellow and finally there is often an exquisite green that always reminded me of my favourite apple green pencil crayon from school days. On many nights during the six weeks on either side of June 21 when the sun barely goes down, and you can read a book outside at midnight! The northern sky in winter can draw one deep into the universe where you may experience a beauty, holiness, wonder and awesomeness that is hard to express.   I found it led me to an awareness of Peace and Spirit.

Oh, yes, I'm going back. You know, there really is, I found out, as Robert Service wrote, "the call of the north".

———◆———

I WENT NORTH WITH MY WEDDING CAKE AND FLOWERS IN HAND

By Muriel Hall

Life in the North, for me, remains the favourite period of my life to date.

It began in 1943, during the War. My finance Bill had been transferred north to Fort Resolution on Great Slave Lake in May of that year, leaving me behind in Edmonton. As we stood on the platform of the railway station saying goodbye, we had no idea of when we might see each other again. This was wartime and we all accepted whatever came our way. Bill was with the Royal Canadian Signals who were providing communication by radio throughout the N.W.T. and Yukon.

Shortly after Bill arrived in Fort Resolution, he rented a small house from the local sawmill owner who only used it as an office when he came into the settlement for mail and supplies. Thus our future plans began to evolve.

I would leave my job in Edmonton, ship my belongings and furniture, from my furnished apartment, north by rail to Waterways and down river from there to Fort Resolution by boat. As this would take a month, I went home to my family for that period, to have a very special visit before flying off into the Great Northern Unknown to get married and make our first home.

The big day to fly North arrived in early October 1943. I left Edmonton airport with our wedding cake in one hand and my flowers in the other.

We flew to Fort Smith by CP Air Boeing where I was met by a Signals couple stationed there and they drove me by jeep to the dock where I transferred to a small Norseman plane on floats. There were only three of us to go aboard - the other two were Catholic nursing sisters returning to Resolution. We climbed aboard and sat on mailbags and other freight as the plane took off for the final leg of our journey.

Landing on Great Slave Lake

The Sisters were anxious and said, "Oh, I hope we make it this time!". This comment made me feel very concerned, as this was my first flight. I asked them why and they said they had tried twice before to land but smoke from the forest fires was too thick for visibility to land. At this point I began to wonder what I was undertaking. But all went well, it was a bumpy flight but being a novice I didn't know what to expect until it happened and then it was too late to worry about it.

We landed in the waters of Great Slave Lake and taxied up to the dock. This was Fort Resolution, I realized, as I peeked out of the aircraft's small windows. Someone put a plank out to the pontoon over which we climbed out onto shore and slowly made our way up to the dock. The sisters managed just fine with their long skirts so I felt I could too, even though I wondered if I slipped into the lake would I drown before I made it to shore.

There were many people down at the dock to meet the plane. Little did I realize at the time the excitement created by a young bride-to-be arriving in their small settlement. (After four years living there I came to know what a rare occasion it was for them). The people were marvelous and everyone wanted to help with wedding arrangements. I found upon arrival that our wedding licence had not yet arrived, so we had to wait before we could set a date.

It was nearing freeze-up so we were anxious to have the wedding before that happened - I began to wonder if I might have to get a job at the Hudson's Bay or elsewhere as you did not live together in those days.

Next, the Anglican minister who was to have married us was taken ill and was flown out to Edmonton. So now what? As ours was a Catholic Mission Village, Bill talked to the priests there and one young American father happily agreed to marry us in a civil ceremony, providing his bishop in Montreal gave him permission.

Radio telegrams flew and permission was finally granted. Now to wait for the licence! It finally arrived - it was by now 12 days since my arrival. We all flew into action. The date was set for two days later, so we worked half the night preparing food and decorating the station home. I had specifically grown my nails for the big day, but I ended up losing most of them while grating and chopping cabbage for the salad! When I first arrived we had stuck the stems of my flowers into a potato and put that into the refrigerator to try and keep them alive. It was to be an evening wedding and sure enough by 7:30 p.m. on October 20, 1943 we were ready.

All the residents of Fort Resolution were there. Dr. Riopel gave me his arm and escorted me down the stairs to where Bill waited supported by the chap who was in charge of the Signal Station. His wife was my attendant and the doctor's wife played the little field organ loaned to us by the American army boys who were stationed there at this time. Our group consisted of our RCMP sergeant, his wife and two constables, a long-time resident and free-trader George Pinsky, wife Mary, the Hudson Bay manager and his wife, the man in charge of the airport (being built at the time) his wife and two teenage daughters and son, as well as our doctor and his wife and our Signals couple. We felt very honoured that everyone wanted to join us.

The service was shorter than a Catholic wedding and Father Gilles was just as nervous as Bill and I. (We have now been married 55 years and Father Gilles has never once missed remembering us on our anniversary.)

Since I had grown up on a farm in Alberta I knew fairly well how to adapt and cope with this new life. There was no electricity, running water or refrigeration and our only heat was from a wood burning cook stove and heater. Some mornings in that first winter we were mighty cold in our house. I sent out to Edmonton for a pair of knee-high felt boots - to wear inside and out. Slacks and sweaters were a must. The Coleman gasoline lamps gave off quite a heat, as well as providing lighting. We had only stovepipe chimneys so were very careful of overnight fires. House fires were disastrous when the lake was frozen over! Drinking water consisted of blocks cut from lake ice, which would last all summer in a sawdust shed.

The first home for Muriel and Bill Hall, at Fort Resolution, in 1943

The Army (to which the Signal Core was attached) provided us with food rations and everything came in tins - butter, bacon, meats, all vegetables, fruits and powdered milk, all shipped in by rail and boat. Eggs came in 30 dozen cases all having been dipped in water glass to keep out the air and maintain some freshness. By spring I was cracking them all very gingerly - some could get very high.

I baked our bread and as the overnight yeast aged I was not always sure how well the loaves would rise. One particular night I put the dough that was in the large mixing pan into towels and then wrapped' it all in a heavy buffalo coat (which was winter issue for the government men to wear) to keep it warm. The fire must have heated more than usual because the next morning I awoke to find one Buffalo coat stuffed with dough - the arms of the coat were even outstretched! I had some job, I can tell you, scraping dough out of the lining.

Our social life was great. We all took turns, once a week in the winter, having everyone over for bridge and other card games followed by lunch and coffee. Dinner parties were frequent and at Christmas we all ordered turkeys from Yellowknife. For Christmas Day the community divided into two groups for the dinners and those Sundays following. No one tired of these dinners, as turkey was much preferred to canned meats. Occasionally we could buy caribou or moose from a local hunter; those meals were special treats.

Summer months with the lovely long days and evenings allowed us to play tennis until all hours of the night, ending up at someone's home for coffee and snacks. The flies and mosquitoes that plagued us there were less numerous in the evenings and we all covered up and used mosquito coils to defend ourselves. Days were exciting when groups of survey men with their students came in to spend their summer doing fish studies on the lake. They gave us fresh conversation and some were terrific tennis players, keeping us on our toes. The annual dentists' visits were also looked forward to, believe it or not.

One year after our wedding, daughter Audrey was born in the local hospital, the first white baby born there in many years. The sisters who kept me in the hospital for 10 days treated me like a queen. The baby was never neglected or allowed to cry as one Sister after another would pick her up and rock her. She was a healthy eight-pound, four-ounce girl born to a mom who had become a healthy overweight woman, who thought once baby arrived I could magically return to my former size and weight. What a shock when I arrived home to find I could only fit into my maternity clothes!

With Dr. Riopel's care and my weekly bundle of fresh rhubarb from his garden to keep me healthy my northern pregnancy seemed flourishing to my health. Consequently, one year from the date of my arrival I desperately sent an order outside (thanks to Eaton's catalogue) for a new red suit, which would fit me.

Our good friend Irene Johnston, the Hudson's Bay manager's wife, helped me over those 'new mother' hurdles for those first nervous weeks. Needless to say, our baby Audrey progressed beautifully with all that literally pure air, disease free in the cold weather. Once she was able to stand, we kept her in a crib with a wooden base over

Muriel, taking baby Audrey for a stroll in a northern baby buggy, in 1944

a mattress to keep her off the cold floor. We mastered many innovations there to stay comfortable. There was no phoning home to mother in those days from that remote community.

We lived in Fort Resolution from 1943 to 1947 and during that time I experienced a couple of challenging events.

The Hudson Bay paid for their manager's children to fly out to Vancouver to attend private schools. One year the relief manager was unable to come in so our local manager asked me to manage the store for him while he took their son to his school in Vancouver. I was to provide the native families with supplies needed when they came in off their trap lines and take their furs and label them for the storeroom and keep records of the transactions. I am not sure what these families thought when they entered the store to find this strange woman behind the counter.

They grouped themselves inside the door and after discussion in their native language, which of course I did not understand, they came to the counter and we muddled through. I think everyone went away with the supplies they wanted. I had worked in retail in Edmonton so basically knew the main things - the cash register, making up the bills and statements of furs received, even though I didn't know a mink from a marten! I left that puzzle for the manager.

The Canadian government brought in family allowance in 1946 and our doctor, who was also the Indian agent, asked me to help sort out and record the native families in his territory. This proved to be one huge challenge. Many families had the same last name but were not related. To list them in their families was difficult, especially with the families who lived in outlying areas. We worked on this for three months before it was completed to our satisfaction.

Treaty Indians were to receive vouchers, whereas the others would receive family allowance cheques. Living in the North gave us a real respect for the people around us. We were all different and had our faults, but we learned to overlook these in favour of the good points that we each had.

Kindness and sense of family pulled us together in rough situations. One woman, a long time resident, was an inspiration to me. She never spoke an unkind word of anyone and always came up with a kind word if anyone had a criticism in her company. She set an example for me I have never forgotten. She was a very strong influence on our little community. Bill and I were 'the youngsters' there, only 23 years old when we married so everyone took us 'under their wing'. We were very lucky even though we did not have all the material things.

Since I knew how to sew I made clothes and household articles (I had brought my sewing machine with me). One lady taught me how to cut hair so I not only cut my husband's hair but also the RCMP constables and thereby got a lot of practice.

When my daughter was born I had been doing our laundry on a good old scrub-board in a galvanized washtub. The RCMP boys had a push-pull wooden machine complete with a screw-on hand turned wringer that they decided I had to use with a new baby. How I blessed them!

I don't really know what I expected to find when I first came North, I only knew I had been given a chance to join Bill in what he lived through and I wanted to share that with him. What a joy to be young and ready to tackle anything!

I just took each day as it came, and this ended up totaling four great years as one of the northern pioneers in those days.

In our last year there, I developed a severe pain and had to be airlifted to Yellowknife for surgery in the Con Mine hospital. While recovering there the Con Mine Bunkhouse burned on Christmas Eve and those of us who were well on our way to recovery were sent out to local families to leave beds free for the men who were victims of that awful fire. I will never forget the chaos in the hospital that night. Friends came early Christmas Day to take me to their home until I was ready to fly back to Fort Resolution.

I had only been home a couple of days when Bill became ill on New Year's Day with what seemed to be flu. Two days later he had become delirious and was running a very high fever. The doctor had gone 'out' for the holiday season. I went over to the Mission Hospital to get the matron to come and see Bill. I was very frightened. She examined him and found a red streak on his leg and cleverly recognized that he had strep poisoning that was caused by a blistered heel. She had the new miracle drug 'penicillin' in her little black bag so immediately gave him the first shot in the hip and said she would be back on a regular basis to give more injections. Then she went to the radio station and asked the chap in charge to notify headquarters in Edmonton that a doctor was needed immediately as Bill was far too ill to be moved.

The army arranged for the assistant Yellowknife doctor to fly in and treat Bill at home. We had an anxious 48 hours waiting for him and felt we could lose Bill. But thanks to the marvelous help of that little nursing sister, her accurate diagnosis and follow-up visits with penicillin shots plus the doctor's attendance and stay with us until Bill could be moved to a hospital, it turned out well. The RCMP came with their dog team and we packed Bill into the sled in the house and then the RCMP men lifted it outdoors and hooked it up to the dog team and moved it to the hospital. We had survived!

Illness in the North in those years was the most worrisome part of living there, especially in the very small communities. Bill's illness was my most difficult situation in four years there.

Muriel and Bill in 1944 at Fort Resolution

We left Fort Resolution in the summer of 1947 and spent 17 months in Edmonton, before Bill was again posted North.

This time it was to Port Radium on Great Bear Lake, the site of the Eldorado Radium Mine. By now we had a second daughter, this one born in Edmonton.

Due to the sudden illness of the wife of the man Bill was to replace in Port Radium, Bill was sent there on only two weeks notice. So I had to sell our new house and arrange for the move up to join him. This time was much easier as the girls and I were flown in on the Eldorado Mining company plane. This plane flew in freight and supplies and flew out the ore from the mine. We passengers sat on row seats while the supplies were piled down the centre.

The girls and I arrived in Port Radium March 17 in time to attend the St. Patrick's dance put on by the social committee. This gave me a chance to meet all our neighbours as everyone attended special events. Baby sitters were never a problem to find as so many young men from the mine were happy to spend an evening in our home enjoying home cooked goodies and listening to recordings for a change from the bunkhouse.

This was such a luxurious life compared to our first northern home. We lived in a government house, complete with steam heat (from the mine), electricity, all appliances, running water and a full bathroom. Bill was a key person in the community so it was our pleasant duty to do whatever we could to enhance living in the North. Entertaining was a big part of life and I never cooked as much before nor since as I did up North.

Fresh foods, fruits and vegetables and milk were flown in every week, as well as meat and poultry. We missed getting these only during fall freeze-up and the spring break-up when we had to wait for the ice to break up so the boats could again navigate the lake across to Sawmill Bay where the summer airport was located. Small floatplanes could also land at the dock in the summer.

There was a super group of people living here, all employed by Eldorado with the exception of the RCMP constable, the Royal Bank manager, the schoolteacher and ourselves. We never lacked for activities. The mine provided a curling rink; movies and we could plan many activities with support from the company management. We really enjoyed a happy, fun-filled time here; everyone did his or her share to make it that way.

We had a company hospital here, complete with a doctor and two nurses, so illness was well looked after as well as babies being born. With so many young men, the nurses, teachers and office stenos had a busy social life and many marriages resulted.

Because of the nature of the mine many interesting visitors flew in from all over, which kept conversation lively, and interests varied. As radio reception was not dependable we all accumulated large collections of musical recordings.

We gals produced many handicrafts on winter afternoons. Someone would find a new craft when they were out on holiday and bring it back for us to learn. Entertaining was a large part of our lives there, hardly a night would pass that we didn't have someone in for coffee, bridge games or dinner parties. In summer with its almost continuous daylight we had to remind ourselves we had to go to bed! We played tennis at midnight in mid-summer and to get our daughters to bed and asleep at a decent hour we ordered heavy room darkening blinds for all our bedroom windows. Winter of course was a complete opposite with the lights on all day and the sun hardly making it into view during December and January. We hiked a great deal, climbing over the rocks and walking on the lovely smooth ice in winter.

Joan, age 4, and Audrey, 8 years old, at Port Radium in 1952

Again I was a barber while in Port Radium and we ladies gave each other home permanents. I did a lot of sewing and each spring made both daughters and myself dresses to match. We even recovered furniture to brighten up our homes.

I was lucky enough, with the curling team, to fly to Yellowknife twice to represent Radium in the Ladies Winter Curling Bonspiel. These were really 'fun trips'. We left all our household and motherly duties behind and were so welcomed by the Yellowknife ladies. We curled nearly all night, or so it seemed.

We lived in Port Radium from March

1949 to September 1953, 4 1/2 years of wonderful living, making our own fun and pleasure. These northern years coming early in our life together gave us a very close relationship both as a couple and family in depending on each other and finding our own ways through many experiences. Little did we realize the impact the early years would have on the years to come and the solid foundation we had built together.

I can honestly say I never felt deprived up North, even though we did miss the fresh foods in our first home and shopping was non-existent. But we were all in the same 'boat' so did not worry about it. We made our own entertainment and had a great time doing it. The friendships I developed there have lasted through the years and that was the most rewarding part of my Northern life.

The saddest experience in Port Radium was the drowning of two little eight-year-old boys in a small lake back of the camp. They had gone there to explore, found a small boat, apparently climbed in and it overturned. They had asked our daughter and her school friends to go with them but the girls didn't go. When the boys were missing for supper the girls told their parents where they had gone. When the bodies were found every effort was made to revive them but it was too late. This terrible tragedy left us all stunned with grief for these two families.

Overall, those precious years North of 60 will always be my favourite. The most memorable events being our wedding and the birth of our eldest daughter. Even now, 50 plus years later, our happiest times seem to be when we get together with fellow ex-northerners and reminisce about those early days. The Arctic Luncheon twice a year during Victoria is a perfect opportunity.

To have lived in "The Land of the Midnight Sun" has been a special privilege.

———◆———

CHICKEN CHARLIE

By Jean Hodgkinson

I'd like to tell you a little about my time in the North. We lived there almost 13 years from 1958 to 1972, with two years "outside" '67-'69 when my husband was on Educational Leave.

We lived in five different places during that time - Fort Chimo, Frobisher Bay (now called Iqaluit), Inuvik, Fort Smith and Whitehorse. My husband Ron worked as an administrator with the Federal Department of Indian and Northern Development.

I went North as a bride, excited at the prospect of living among the Eskimos (now referred to as Inuit). We had to cross the Kokjuak River by dog team to reach the settlement of Fort Chimo (now called Kokjuak) in the Ungava Bay area of Northern Quebec.

I was charmed when all the Eskimos turned out to shake my hand and welcome me with big grins to their tiny village. In those days they did not speak English.

My most vivid memory of those days was when I flew south to have my first baby. To get to the airport we traveled by dog team when I was 7 1/2 months pregnant. It was pretty hilarious when I struggled up, through deep snow, the hills that were too steep for the dogs to pull me on the komatik. And riding over the pressure ridges of the river ice, caused by the tides, was far from comfortable. But worst of all was the length of time it took - 4 1/2 hours of discomfort from an increasingly full bladder in late pregnancy!

When I returned with a one-month-old baby, an Eskimo woman carried him on her back for the dog team trip as we perched precariously atop the baggage on the komatik. My heart sank as I saw my baby disappear from view in her parka, and I was relieved to see him still breathing when we reached our destination. Again villagers turned out to greet us, and each one touched the baby's head.

Fort Chimo was the most southerly, but the most isolated of all the places we lived in the North. In the second year the settlement was moved across the river to the airport side, where living was easier.

In the old settlement there were only five white families, no roads or vehicles, no fresh meat, fruit or vegetables, so it was quite a change from city life. When we walked around the settlement, we often carried sticks to deter any loose huskies that looked hungry.

I had to learn immediately how to bake bread, which was no mean feat for someone who had little experience in cooking. But I'm proud to say I never had a failure.

Our little home in Chimo was no palace! In the winter the water froze on the floor if one attempted to mop it. Food supplies for the first year were mainly cans left over from the construction crew that had been there before us - there was lots of jello powders, corn-flakes, Bird's Custard powders and dehydrated vegetables. One learned quickly to improvise when trying to follow a recipe! But we did have several cases of lobster and crab.

Water was pumped into tanks in each house from the river, and was pure enough to drink. It had to be pumped when the tide changed, to avoid getting salty water. Fort Chimo was about 20 miles from Ungava Bay, but the tides were still 15-20 feet high.

In summer clouds of mosquitoes surrounded us. In the fall and winter the Northern Lights were just glorious.

A few experiments were carried out in Fort Chimo. We incubated hen's eggs in the house and the chicks ran around in one of the rooms until they got too big and smelly. Then an Eskimo called "Chicken Charlie" looked after them, and all in the settlement got an egg or two every few days. Then geese were raised for a while. None of these experiments were very successful.

Jean, with son Eric, in Fort Chimo, near Ungava Bay, 1959

Many interesting people came to visit my husband, most of who stayed with us, as there certainly were no hotels available. Among these were federal government officials, scientists and even some newspaper reporters who were so impressed by our northern hospitality and home-made bread that they mentioned us in a book one of them wrote.

I enjoyed moving about in the North every few years. I felt to stay longer than two or three years in a small community was too much. One needed the stimulation of a change. Often we met the same people in more than one community. People become very close in the North, depending on each other, helping each other out and always eagerly meeting newcomers and making them feel at home. This was particularly so in the Northwest Territories. Whitehorse in the Yukon was bigger and seemed less personal. But Yukon had other advantages - so much beauty in the mountains all around, so many places to drive to, so much to see and do.

There were a few drawbacks to living in the North. Our children did not get to know their relatives at all well in the early years. We all missed out on cultural things, and a variety of other things. And later, it was not easy for wives to get careers going after years in the North. But when it came time to leave the North, we had three very unhappy children and it took them quite a while to fit into the more sophisticated schools and social life in the city.

But we all feel so enriched by our experiences in the north, and feel very lucky to have been there in the relatively early days. We have friends all over Canada now whom we knew in the North. When we see them after many years, it is as if we had just seen them yesterday.

There was a time when I was almost widowed a few months after my wedding when Ron tackled a big storm in Ungava Bay in a 26 foot Cape-Islander boat; and another challenge when our 2 1/2 year old son was bitten by a husky in Inuvik. And then there was the time we went for a Sunday drive from Fort Smith in -20C weather and our vehicle broke down! There was no other around and we had a baby and two small children and hadn't told anyone where we were going.

Equally foolish was a drive I made with a friend from Fort Smith to Hay River. It snowed hard and we ended up in a ditch in a whiteout. The only vehicle we saw on that trip was the big truck that came by in the next few minutes and pulled us out.

And so our adventures went on until we finally returned to the south. I feel as if there were enough to write a whole book about them. Who knows, maybe I will.

———◆———

EXCERPTS OF LETTERS FROM A NURSE IN INUVIK

By Mary Johnson

INUVIK, N.W.T., December 1961

This year the time for Christmas letters seem to have come earlier than usual. Friends often ask what we find to do here in our spare time. Sometimes I'm inclined to reply "What spare time?" Time passes so quickly that often I have quite the job getting my chores done. I have been helping with one of the Girl Guide companies. There are four companies in town and four Brownie packs - this takes quite a bit of time as I have had to relearn much of the material that I have forgotten since my teens!

On Thursday nights I baby sit for the RCMP pilot and his wife. Then there are craft classes, church activities, dances, concerts and meetings of various sorts, as well as outdoor activities such as curling, skiing hiking, and trips by plane and bombardier to the outlying communities. So you see, we never lack for anything to do; the difficulty is in choosing.

What is Inuvik like? It is difficult to describe. The main impression is one of colour. All the buildings are painted in different bright shades that make them stand out against the green background in summer and the white snow in winter. Because of

Mary Johnson at Tuktoyaktuk, early 1960s

the permafrost, no building has a basement and the majority of them are built up on stilts. This is to prevent the heat from the buildings melting the permafrost. This happened once at Aklavik a town not too far away.

Inuvik is situated on the easternmost channel of the Mackenzie River Delta, which is approximately 40 miles wide and 100 miles long. It is a vast area of channels, lakes and islands that you need to see to appreciate. There is enough timber in the Delta, which is in the tree line, to warrant a sawmill at Aklavik and yet, one only has to go 3 miles or so to see the real Arctic tundra.

Although Inuvik is 150 miles within the Arctic Circle, the annual snowfall is only 8-10 inches. Temperatures may drop to 60 below zero in the winter, but this last summer it went up to 85 above and this is not unusual. The mosquitoes are thick in summer, but 24 hours of sunlight for 5 weeks makes it very pleasant. Right now the days are getting very short and soon we will have no sun at all for five weeks, however, there will be twilight for about two hours each day and the moonlight on the snow will make it light enough to get around.

During my time here I have visited Tuktoyaktuk on the Arctic Ocean, Herschel Island which is just off the Arctic coast of the Yukon (which, incidentally was carpeted with flowers when we were there in July - so beautiful then but so bleak in winter!) Cape Parry, a dewline (Distant Early Warning) station above the 70th parallel where I stayed with two Eskimo babies whom I was escorting home to Cambridge Bay. I have been over to Aklavik a number of time and also visited Arctic Red River and Fort McPherson which are small communities not too far from Inuvik.

February 1962

The weather was unseasonably warm for January in Inuvik. It was 25F, but winds were blowing and gusting to 40 mph. Due to the high winds the plane from Edmonton spent the night at Norman Wells and was expected to arrive in Inuvik about 10:30 on this Saturday morning. The smaller planes were unable to fly in this weather.

At the Inuvik General Hospital it appeared to be a typically quiet Saturday morning. the Office Manager had come in to attend to some outstanding business. About 9:30 an Eskimo appeared in the front hall and quietly informed him there was a sick man 22 miles away in 'the bush'. The nurse came and helped to get the whole story.

Our informant, Don, had found out about the sick man on a chance visit to one of the trappers' winter quarters. The man, Jimmy, had been vomiting for three days and complained of a sore stomach.

"Why didn't you bring him with you, Don?"

"He was too weak and kept fainting. I didn't like to bring him because the trail was hard going."

We then discovered Don had started out for Inuvik with his dog team in the middle of the night to get help. The camp was only 22 miles away but it had taken him four and a half hours of hard going. The winds were strong and in some places the snow was above his knees and he had to break trail for the dogs. Asked if he was tired, he replied , "I'm a little sleepy".

The doctor was notified and arrived to discuss the problem with Don. Among other things he told us Jimmy had eaten meat from a drowned whale and this was probably the cause of his trouble. The doctor said it was essential to bring the sick man to the hospital as soon as possible. But how was it to be accomplished? The weather ruled out the use of a small plane. The deep snow and time involved made using a dog team impractical.

The only solution seemed to be a bombardier, but these are scarce in Inuvik. A bombardier is a larger forerunner of the skidoo, a tracked snow vehicle almost reminiscent of a tank. The doctor phoned Northern Affairs and found that their vehicle was out of town but they told him that John Lambert at Reindeer Station planned to come to Inuvik by bombardier that same afternoon. If we could contact him he would probably be willing to pick up Jimmy and bring him to the hospital.

We turned to Don again to try and find out just where the sick man was situated.

"He's 22 miles away in the bush."

"In which direction?"

"Near Reindeer Station."

"On the direct route between here and Reindeer Station?"

"No, quite a way off the route - he's at the camp on the lake."

As this whole area is a network of rivers and lakes, this information wasn't much use to us greenhorns! We eventually elicited the information that the camp was near Rufus River and that John Lambert would know where it was anyway!

The doctor phoned CBC Radio and asked if a message could be broadcast a number of times to John Lambert and we all hoped he would hear it before he left for Inuvik.

There was nothing to do now but wait. The day passed slowly - the weather remained much the same.

About 3:30 p.m. a bombardier drew up in front of the hospital with Jimmy safely aboard. Mr. Lambert helped us to lift him on to a stretcher, and after short examination in the Outpatient Department, he was taken directly to the ward and made warm and comfortable. Mr. Lambert told us he had heard the message on the radio and had gone directly to the camp that was in the middle of the lake. Twice they had become suck in the snow but eventually got near enough to move the man by toboggan to the bombardier. We thanked Mr. Lambert for his part in the adventure, something he seemed to take all in a day's work.

Meanwhile Jimmy appeared to have stopped vomiting, though his stomach was still sore. He was given intravenous feedings to help make up for all the fluid he had lost. He appeared to be very glad to be in a warm bed. He denied eating "bad" whale meat and didn't know what could have caused his vomiting. His family had been with him at the camp and none of them had been sick.

On further examination he was found to be suffering from acute laryngitis and pneumonia at the base of his left lung. However, two days later he was sitting up cheerfully in bed, well on his way to recovery.

Twenty-two miles sounds like a short journey, particularly in this part of the country where distance is counted in hundred of miles, but the weather and the location turned this short distance into a hazardous journey.

Two years later - March 1964

This is my fourth year in Inuvik and I still find it both fascinating and frustrating. Yet it remains my favourite assignment in 18 years with Medical Services. Despite the frustrations, it was a stimulating learning experience. Where else would I have had the opportunity as a hospital-oriented nurse to spend seven weeks at the nursing station in Tuktoyaktuk?

I made a number of friends in Tuk during that time and had visited now and then on holiday weekends during my time in Inuvik. Easter was early this year and the sea still solidly frozen, but the sun is up for a few hours each day, the temperature is improving and it is pleasant and easy to get around - so Audrey Weir and I decided to go to Tuk for the long weekend. Audrey is our hospital schoolteacher and had previously spent seven years in Tuk.

We took the early morning flight and after lunch attended the English Good Friday service at the little Anglican log church that was held this afternoon - the Eskimo services were always held in the morning.

An oil drum wood stove heated the church and extra logs were stored in the porch. As the service was drawing to a close we heard a very distinct rough grating sound, as if someone was dragging the logs from the porch.

The Pokiak children playing with the dogs in Tuktoyaktuk in April 1963. The nursing station is in the background.

However as we came out of the church we noticed vapour rising all along the coast and 200 feet off shore and we all wondered what was happening.

A few hours later we heard via the radio about the Alaskan earthquake - the radiating shock wave was so great that it caused a fissure 6 - 8 inches wide through 5 feet of sea ice. The noise we heard in the church was the grinding of the ice segments as they came together and eventually rejoined. Reflecting later on this incident, we were thankful the earthquake did not occur later in the year after the ice had cleared. Then the Tsunami (tidal wave) would surely have flooded the whole village.

MAGIC AND MYSTERY IN THE LAND OF THE MIDNIGHT SUN

By Marion Langevin

In 1955 I was principal of the Bluesky School in the Fairview, Alberta School Division. The job was very demanding as I also had a full-time class of grades 7,8 and 9. My name was Marion Mayowksi and I was quite content and happy with my achievements and myself. I had just purchased a brand new car and was only about 70 miles from my parents' home.

It was one of those typical spring days in Northern Alberta when the owner of the Bluesky Motel knocked on my classroom door and told me there was a phone call asking if I would accept a teaching position in the Yukon Territory. Without blinking an eyeball I said, "Tell him, 'Yes.'" That started the ball rolling. I had accepted a teaching position at Haines Junction, Mile 1016 on the Alaska Highway.

It was finalized that I was going to a new job in the Yukon so now I had to make preparations for this big move and adventure. I ordered two big trunks from Eaton's and had them go to my parents address. When I arrived several weeks later, my Dad asked why I had ordered the big trunks. When I told them I was going to Yukon to teach, they were really dumbfounded. I was told in no uncertain terms that what I was doing was dumb and absolutely stupid as there were nothing but Eskimos and Indians along this terrible trail they called the Alaska Highway.

"Too late," I said, "I have to go." My parents made me sell my car, as there was no way they would let me drive up the Alaska Highway. My new adventure stirred up a lot of talk in our small community of Nampa, Alberta.

By mid August my travel vouchers arrived, the trip was being paid for by the department of education in Yukon. I met Shirley Sillers from Estevan, Saskatchewan in Edmonton. She too was going to teach at Haines Junction. She was very tall, 5' 10" compared to my 5' 1". (We were dubbed Mutt and Jeff on arrival in Haines Junction).

We flew to Whitehorse - complete with suits, hats, gloves and high heels - and were met at the airport by the superintendent of schools, Harry Thompson. Next day we were on the bus heading for Haines Junction, a 100-mile trip. We were excited and a little scared. Finally we arrived and as the bus pulled up by the Fairdale Store where the community was there to meet and greet 'the new teachers'.

We discovered that our 'school' and living accommodation were within the North-West Highway Compound, an army maintenance camp for the Alaska Highway. We were in the middle of the housing complex and my classroom was actually the army recreation centre with one corner partitioned off for the canteen. This would be most interesting, I thought.

I was the head teacher, grades 4 to 9 consisting of about 21 students, and the recreation centre doubled as my classroom.

Our apartment also proved to be interesting; it was sandwiched in between the rec hall and the other classroom (all in one building). Shirley and I learned to love our little Hansel and Gretel abode. We had two sawhorses and plywood for a table, a wood-burning cook stove, a couple of chairs, two army cots and a bottomless easy chair. Every time you sat down the bottom fell through! Our shower was in the kitchen and several times one of us was caught while in there by someone appearing at the door. But we settled in quickly and were excited and happy with our new adventure.

Haines Junction had a population of about 150 people in 1955 and was in the midst of building a new community hall and fire hall. A curling rink had just been put up. There was always a lot to see and do, once a week a film came up the Alaska Highway and was shown at each camp along the highway.

Once a month there was a dance, various people in the community took turns putting on the entertainment.

By Christmas time we had met and were dating a couple of fellows. I was going with the local Forest and Game Warden, Joe Langevin, and Shirley was dating one of the RCMP. There were dances, a Bonspiel and other diversions going on up and down the highway and there seemed to be no restrictions on using the government vehicles. We were always on 'patrol'.

I had planned to stay only one year, but by the end of May cupid had done his work and Joe and I were engaged. Our wedding at Haines Junction was planned for August 25th, 1956. I flew home for the summer and got ready for the 'wedding'. The wedding was the first wedding in the little Catholic Church, and it was truly an Alaska Highway affair. We had over 300 people and the community of Haines junction organized the whole thing. They even painted the community hall for the event. We flew off to Juneau, Alaska for our honeymoon.

I taught the next two years and then our first son Brian was born, in November 1959. Son number two, Gerry, was added to the family in 1961. As Joe had already spent 11 1/2 years at Haines Junction we were moved to Dawson City, Yukon later that year.

Before our move to Dawson City we had a very scary experience. We were camped out in our new home-built camper at the Takhini River when there was a knock at the door and someone was asking for gas. Joe went out as I was getting the boys settled down for the night. Then I heard someone say something about money - I looked out there were two guys staging a holdup - they had a gun on Joe and were going to tie him up and rob us. Joe gave them his wallet (with the grand sum of $22 in it) plus his game warden badge. They thought the badge was a police officer badge so decided to take something out of the truck engine to immobilize us. Then they left. My husband flagged down a trucker and in short order the culprits were apprehended by the RCMP. One of our assailants received another 10 years in custody, which added to his already long criminal record.

We moved to Dawson City in October 1961, living in the old Commissioner's Residence on 7th Avenue.

The house was old, cold and rundown. The electrical wiring was scary with most of its insulation gone. We still had battery crank phones and all the light bulbs were 40- or 60-watt as electricity was expensive.

It was supplied to the City of Dawson by the Yukon Gold Corporation, which was mining the creeks of the Klondike using dredges powered by electricity.

Joe and Marion Langevin, married at Haines Junction, August 25, 1956

I remember a fellow coming to the door and telling us to turn on the bleeders. As we had no idea what this was, he said he'd turn them on. It turned out it was a system set up so water kept circulating slowly in the pipes to keep them from freezing. Well, he turned them on on a Saturday. Sunday morning I ventured down to the makeshift basement to get a can of milk for breakfast. I didn't put the light on as the wiring was very poor and sparks would run along the bare wires. As I was about to step of the stairs - kersplash - I was in water up to my waist, about to be struck by a case of toilet paper floating by. What a mess! Flour, soap, groceries and all of the boxes yet to be unpacked!

On December 29 the temperature dropped to -80 F. We ventured out because one of the Forestry fellows was being married. Some people drove the 350 miles from Whitehorse to the wedding and brought fresh flowers!

I was soon teaching home economics part-time at the high school, three afternoons a week, which I did for the next four or five years. When both boys were in school I went back to teaching full-time from 1965-1980. I loved my work and involvement in the community and our social life was just great.

I also became a member of the Nutty Club, a group of women who wrote a bimonthly newsletter called the Klondike Korner. This was great fun. We printed and mailed it out on Thursday nights and always retired to the local pub to wash away the stamp glue. (This newsletter originated during the war when soldiers were kept abreast of happenings at home).

Curling was the main sport and we all curled. One weekend we hosted a 40 rink Bonspiel on two sheets of ice. No one went to bed. We billeted visiting curlers, ran the snack bar, did the potluck dinners, did the banquet, curled in the spiel, gave out prizes, and did the decorating and clean-up at the end. Lights went out early on Monday evening after that weekend.

In 1971 my husband retired so we moved out of government housing and into our own brand new 12 X 71-foot trailer. We cut logs and built a beautiful log home on 2nd Avenue (Paradise Alley during the gold rush days). There were two bawdyhouses across the street, Ruby's and Bombay Peggy's, but by now both had been shut down. We also bought the old original Dawson Hardware Store (building and contents). We proceeded to tear this down, saving the front facade, and built a beautiful Gold Rush Museum with over 27,000 items. I ran this museum during the summer holidays from 10 am to 9 pm. It wasn't too profitable then, as the tourist trade had not yet come to Dawson.

My husband also bought claims #7 and #8 on the Victoria Gulch on Upper Bonanza Creek and was spending all his time out there prospecting and panning and having fun. This was placer gold mining and we were finding gold. I loved gold panning and resented being stuck in town at the museum. We decided to sell the museum to the city so all my free time in the summer holidays was on Victoria Gulch. Some of our good friends also had staked claims on Victoria Gulch so we had all kinds of parties and fun. Every Saturday night we drove into town to go to Diamond Tooth Gertie's Gambling Hall. We often ended up on the stage doing some silly skit or performance. This was the life! No TV, no phone, no radio!

We always had plenty of company out on the creek and everyone always went home with the gold they had panned. I set up my own gold mining operation, a sluice box, waterline and plenty of shoveling. One summer I got 5 ounces of gold on my own. My husband and partner had gone on into more serious mining and we were enjoying life to the utmost. Who cared if our fingernails were gone and we had blisters from shoveling. Finding gold was our goal - on a fun and hobby basis only, of course.

We came into town to do the laundry, ironing, shopping and visiting. We picked lots of berries and made jams and jellies and had so much fun.

In 1984, Dawson City hosted the first World Gold Panning Championship. Joe and I decided to compete. Joe came in first in world senior Competition and I came in third in the women's division. What a victory! As I had never even competed in gold panning before, this was really something to crow about.

We bought a home on Vancouver Island in 1980 and spent the winters there. But we headed north by mid April and lived on the creek and mined and traveled to Alaska and Inuvik and then with the first freeze up we packed up and drove back to our home near Parksville.

My husband still goes up to our claim on California Gulch for six months, but I now stay behind to look after our property here. I go back to Dawson City for six weeks or so every summer.

Dawson City has really changed. It is now a national historic site and Parks Canada does the restoration and organizes the tours. Many buildings have been saved and restored and are in use today. Tourism is the main industry now. Diamond Tooth Gertie's is in full swing with black-jack, poker, roulette and slot machines. The Palace Grand Theatre presents live performances and the Ghost of Robert Service appears at the old Service home daily to relate his story and recite his poems. The Spell of the Yukon is probably Service's most famous poem and still elicits the magic, mystery and silence of the north.

The best years of my life were spent in Yukon, 33 years in all and I still consider it my home. I will always cherish the memories, good times and friends we made there. Both of our sons are still there so we always have a reason to go back. This is truly the land of magic and mystery and the midnight sun.

———◆———

Marion Langevin passed away in 1997 at the age of 65.

"GUESS WHAT!"

By Marion Lysyk

Being the wife of an RCMP member, you never knew just what to think when your husband came home and said, "Guess what?" Too often it meant a transfer - leaving a place you have grown accustomed to and had made good friends and so on.

Early in 1951 my husband came home with the 'guess what?" phrase, and I learned we were transferred "North" - to some place called Hay River. About all he could tell me was its location: on the south shore of Great Slave Lake. But I found out nothing about a house, shopping, other residents, etc.

It didn't take long before our things were put into storage in Regina and off we went with some pictures, clothing and a few personal items.

What an experience it was driving north from Peace River for two days over a dusty highway, still under construction in some areas! And what a surprise to arrive in Hay River to find there were no married quarters and no houses for rent! We moved into the hotel, which because of a flood that spring, had rooms that had doors that would not close, let alone lock. The flood or such proportion that canoes were used in the lobby!

The settlement consisted of a large Indian population and people who were, for the most part, involved in a large fishing industry. The noise level in our room became intense as the evening wore on: our room was above the beer parlor. Of course my husband was not in the room with me very much until the wee hours of the morning because law and order had to be looked after. What I wondered, was I doing living in a hotel room hundreds of miles from so called civilization.

After a few weeks though when one RCMP member left the force and another was transferred out, my husband decided we would move into the furnished quarters used by the single men. No red tape or bureaucracy involved. That was it. The single men would move into an office and I would be required to cook, not just for my husband but the single men too. No red tape or bureaucracy involved in this decision either. Then I discovered I was to cook for the prisoners as well. The two cells were part of the office complex. No protest from me. It beat hotel life!

But I soon found I did not escape the noise. The two cells were separated from our bedroom with a thin wall. As night wore on the drunks filled the cells and the noise became awesome at times. My husband and the men decided they would limit the number of drunks in the cells to 10 - five in each cell minus the number that were serving time.

Any prisoner serving time was on good behavior during the day. Their sentence was "at hard labour". But the labour wasn't too hard - and they did eat well (I thought!). One constable gave me a hard time about serving prisoners lemon meringue pie for dessert.

46

At times the men would be away from the office for quite a while. So guess who was in charge of the prisoners. Sunday afternoon was visitors' day for prisoners. This one Sunday a large shipment of supplies arrived for the detachment. The men were away, so no rest for me. I got the prisoners working sorting out the supplies and then one of the prisoner's parents arrived. But no time for that, the only visiting that could be done was while work was going on. Soon the father got involved in the work too. When my husband got back he didn't really like it that I had put the father to work, but after speaking with the father, he found he had not minded at all, because he got the same good cake and coffee as the prisoners during coffee break.

After a while it seemed I was "'just part of the detachment." Maybe I worked a bit harder. Our kitchen had an icebox (no fridge) that required a block of ice put in daily. A fishing company supplied the ice, but guess who was required to pick it up? Being a couple of miles away I had to use the police car. Also I had to use it for shopping because the Hudson's Bay store was quite far down a dusty road. Soon it was not an unusual sight for people to see this blonde driving a police car all over town. One day, though, my husband and the constable suggested I slow off a bit because they needed the car too. I had just taken an Army Signals wife berry-picking - she knew the best place to go. It happened the place was 60 miles south of Hay River near the Alberta border. We were gone many hours. To make things worse some senior Northern Affairs officials were in town from Ottawa and were with my husband in the police office when I drove by taking the other lady home. Apparently the comment was, "I don't believe it - but I didn't see anything."

At that time houses in Hay River did not have sewage or running water. Water was delivered to a barrel in the corner of the kitchen and sewage was an outdoor 'biffy' or if inside, it was a ''honey bucket' operation.

After being in Hay River for spring, summer and fall, the RCMP decided my husband would be reduced in rank, from corporal to constable. Of course it fell upon me to remove the 'stripes' from all his red tunics, brown tunics, pea jacket, etc. But that was a small part of the story. Within a month I got the "guess what" question and found we were transferred to Fort Smith where my husband would again be a corporal because the Fort Smith Detachment had 12 members, six of whom were involved in death-watch duty guarding a prisoner waiting to be hanged for murder. We had two days to get everything together. A police plane would take us to Fort Smith. But there was the requirement that I sew corporal stripes back on the red tunics, brown tunics and pea jacket before we left. My husband didn't object to my mumbling about the RCMP not really knowing what they were doing.

Fort Smith was quite acceptable. We had a nice house assigned us, located on a golf course, overlooking the main rapids of the Slave River. Also it had hot and cold running water, flush toilet, and a thermostatically controlled oil furnace! And there was more. Quite often a female prisoner was sent to the house to fulfill some of her 'hard labour' sentence. Most were very nice and I became so friendly with some of them that they came back to visit and have tea for a long time after their sentences were completed. Earlier I mentioned the deathwatch over the prisoner who was to be hanged. He had murdered a woman and two children. A hangman flown in from Montreal carried out the sentence in the RCMP compound.

By coincidence our first son was born within an hour of the hanging. This coincidence became more of a coincidence a year later when another prisoner was hanged in the RCMP compound (for murdering his wife) and our second son was born a short time later.

Fort Smith was an enjoyable place to live, as there were lots of nice people to socialize with, three stores to shop in, and enough social functions to make life enjoyable. But enjoying life for too long wasn't part of the RCMP regimen because after 1 1/2 years it was "guess what" again and we were off to Yellowknife where my husband was to be the sergeant in charge of the detachment. (Remember, a year and a half earlier the RCMP reduced him from corporal to constable?)

Yellowknife, 1953, was like returning to big city living - many stores, theatre, modern hospital, parks, beach etc. etc. But one mustn't get too comfortable about anything when you're with our national police force because a year later it was "Guess what?" time again and we were on our way back to Fort Smith where we occupied the same house as before and where we enjoyed life for another year before being transferred "outside" to Saskatoon. Our four-year stint North of 60 provided much to reflect on.

By 1959, we had learned to enjoy life in Ottawa, after having been transferred there after our three-year posting in Saskatoon. But then, you guessed it! "Guess what" time again and this time it was north with a capital "N".

I knew Aklavik was so far north, above the Arctic Circle, that for a period of time in the winter the sun did not rise above the horizon. But I knew little else about it.

By now I had five children, the fifth only a month old. So I suggested to my husband that he go and I remain in Ottawa with the children awaiting his return. He had no reaction either way but he did know that to refuse the posting would mean searching for another job. Anyway, after much thought, a week later I changed my mind. "Ah, what the hell, let's give it a whirl!" I said.

Marion and Ed Lysyk with their five children, above the Arctic Cirle at Aklavik in 1959

Our belongings were put into storage and again we were off with only personal effects, clothing and some pictures. The seven of us drove across Canada from Ottawa to Hay River in a station wagon in 10 days. There we left the station wagon (hoping it would still

48

be there three years later) and flew with Canadian Pacific to Norman Wells. There a police plane picked us up and took us to Aklavik to survey our new home, a new settlement.

Of paramount interest was, of course, our house and its furnishings. I discovered the house to be a small two-bedroom home with beds to accommodate three - one double bed plus a single. But there were seven of us.

One thing you find in northern settlements is that everyone is so kind and helpful. Hearing of our plight the Roman Catholic Mission soon had two upper and lower bunks plus a crib in our house. The crib went in our bedroom and the two double bunks went in the other bedroom. This latter arrangement (with a small bedroom the bunks were close together) provided excellent opportunity for kids to fight on two levels at the same time!

And we were back to a water barrel in the corner of the kitchen and a 'honey bucket' bathroom. I will never forget the terrible sight and odour of the honey bucket when it was taken by a prisoner from the bathroom through our kitchen outside to be emptied each morning while we were having breakfast in our small kitchen.   On the plus side, we did have electricity and an oil furnace.

During the winter the children of course went to school in the dark and came home in the dark.   Everyone waited for that day in February "when the sun came back". That meant a small sliver of sun just peeked over the horizon for a few minutes. From then on it rose higher and higher each day until June at which time it didn't go down below the horizon at all. It was seen 24 hours a day.

Again I had the good fortune of having a female prisoner come to my house periodically to help with housework. A couple of them were "regulars" so we became good friends and I enjoyed their company (it was enjoyable to have them). But they all seemed to have a problem. Each time they were released from the RCMP jail, they celebrated to the extreme resulting in their landing back in jail and serving more time. But they didn't seem to mind too much - they ate well, slept well, and had quite a good time. Again a year later when we were living in Inuvik, the Aklavik lady prisoners always came to my house for a visit whenever they got to Inuvik and I was always glad to see them. At times they insisted on helping me with my housework even though they weren't serving time.

A memorable experience for all us RCMP wives one summer was a three day trip on the RCMP schooner from Aklavik to Tuktoyaktuk and return during which time we saw many whales. I was glad to do this because my husband had previously taken our two oldest sons on a whale-hunting trip and they were rather boastful of having experienced something mother never did. Life has its moments as they say, and I had some at Aklavik.

One frightening experience happened while I was doing some work in the Aklavik house living room and suddenly the whole room filled with smoke. Running to the kitchen where our third son was, I fought smoke pouring out of the oven where I was baking bread. My son had opened the oven door and stuffed numerous plastic toys into it on top of the bread.

Another "smoke" incident couldn't be blamed on any of the children. Our eldest son seemed to get into numerous "tussles" with other kids at school. He wore glasses and that of course was a handicap whenever he got into a fight. At 40 below zero the plastic frames would break at the slightest touch. After a while glue and tape could no longer do the job of keeping them together and I seized the opportunity of flying with him in a police plane to Edmonton for new glasses and frames. I was a smoker and enjoyed a cigarette on the flight. As I was butting out my cigarette in the ashtray it accidentally fell between the canvas along the wall and a cloth wall, which had been put in to protect the main wall from some freight. At any rate, I could not reach the lit butt and before long smoke was billowing out from between the canvas and the wall. It caused excitement. And I am convinced the pilot and the co-pilot, after emptying the fire extinguisher, regarded me as a real turkey! I must say my son and I got a panic thrill out it and I can also say that was the last cigarette I ever smoked in an airplane.

In 1960 my husband's famous "guess what" was mentioned again and I immediately thought we were headed south! There was no sub-division headquarters north of Aklavik. So it had to be south, I thought. Then he explained he would go down in RCMP history as being the last O.C. (Officer-in-Charge) in the Western Arctic sub-division. And where was Western Arctic Division going to be? Just 30 miles east! Inuvik.

Well moving to Inuvik was just fine. We had a large house connected to a utilidor that brought water and heat to our house and took away the sewage. Flush toilets! The perma-frost at Inuvik meant that all buildings were built on top of piles driven into the ground and the buildings had an approximate three foot space between their floor and the ground. Water and sewage couldn't be put underground because the ground was permanently frozen (so it was transferred through pipes raised several feet above ground and covered over in a box-like structure). It did thaw a foot or so in the summer and that permitted some to plant a small garden. Things grow rapidly when the sun shines 24 hours a day!

Inuvik had two large schools, one operated by the Catholic Church and the other by the Anglican Church. Our children went to the Catholic school, belonged to Cubs, were altar boys at the "Igloo" church and generally life was good. The large airport allowed freighter aircraft to bring in fresh produce and frequent flights meant regular mail service. The Bay had a large store; there was a hotel and even a restaurant. With all the amenities I often reflect on how wrong it would have been had I elected to stay in Ottawa.

When we were transferred out of Inuvik it was to Winnipeg where my husband was to be the first Administrative Officer. But when we arrived in Winnipeg we were told that the RCMP were a bit ahead of themselves and wouldn't be setting up that position for another year - but not to worry they'd find another job. That other job was in Ottawa, so off we went, completing the full circle. I had some thoughts about the RCMP and their mind-changing - but I also kept thinking back on the experiences I'd have missed out on had I remained in Ottawa and not had the wonderful experience of living not just north of 60 - but North of the Arctic Circle. It was great!

WE WENT NORTH FOR FIVE YEARS — AND STAYED FOR THIRTY-TWO!

By Dolly Macara

After my husband was discharged from the R.C.A.F. in 1946, he had an offer to go to Yellowknife to open a dry cleaning and laundry plant. Since he had experience in this work he, our daughter and I left the city of Edmonton to venture North. We traveled in a small plane sitting on freight boxes.

At the time, accommodation in Yellowknife was at a premium, but we managed to get one room in an old wooden building, which were kitchen, bedroom and living room all in one.

What I missed most was not having indoor plumbing, I had to get pails of water from the lake, but I made up my mind I had to make the best of it, which was not easy. It was very primitive after coming from the city.

I think the good part of the community in the early days was that there was no discrimination.

All the children played together, the women socialized from all walks of life, from professionals to the most ordinary.

In time, we would go on to have three children. The youngest especially says she is happy she was brought up in the North.

Dolly Macara with her husband and children during the early 1950s in Yellowknife

We thought we would stay five years and ended up staying for 32 years, with no regrets because we made such good friends. It seems no matter where we go we seem to meet a friend from the North.

One humourous memory that stands out in my mind is when my husband and I were downtown on a day when it was very, very cold, about -55 F and an icy cold wind was blowing. We met an Eskimo friend, Abe Ookpik. We said, "It sure is cold," and he said, "Yes, it's even too cold for an Eskimo."

———◆———

THE BLACK HOUSE
IN DAWSON CITY, YUKON

By Betty Mackie

The search for a habitable place in Dawson City in 1950 was on again. We did not have a lot of notice for such a move, but we did have a friend who had just purchased the Black house and was willing to rent it to us. It was by far the most elegant dwelling in town. A three-storey white frame building with a large porch, it was fully furnished but had not been lived in for some time. Most impressive of all was the fact that it had something of a dugout under the house, which housed a large wood-burning furnace. This was made possible by the fact that the house was situated in the south end of town and permafrost was not such a severe problem here.

In its heyday it was the summer residence of George and Martha Black. George Black had served as the Commissioner of the Yukon Territory from 1912 to 1916, was overseas during the First World War, and was an elected Member of Parliament and Speaker of the House. His wife, Martha Louise (Munger) Black, a lady of style and spirit,

Betty Mackie's sketch of the Black house in Dawson City

greatly admired by all and sundry, had joined the Klondike Gold Rush in 1898 and hiked in over the Chilkoot Pass. This legendary couple lived in Whitehorse and I felt bound to try and maintain a certain Northern style while living in what I always thought of as their home.

The house was situated beside Canada's most northerly outdoor swimming pool with water steam-heated directly from the power plant. Between the swimming pool and the front driveway was a hedge of wild roses, which gave off their sweet pungent perfume all summer. Best of all, it had a long very conveniently located clothesline.

Inside, we tried to concentrate what furniture was left behind into the second and third storeys. There were ample large rooms with high ceilings on the main floor to house our growing family. By now we had taken on a single father and his small boy. The father stayed only a short while and then went "out to the gold creeks" to work for the mining company and try to recoup his financial situation. The little boy stayed with us.

Our friend who owned the house wanted to sell any or all of the contents. He made arrangements with me to let people come to view at their leisure and I was to make the sale, as he too had gone "out to the gold creeks" to work.

One morning I had a phone call from the town's best known Madame (Ruby Scott, late of Paris, France) saying she would like to come and look at beds. I was delighted and curious. She arrived with her little dog "Shee-Shee" and tied it to one of the pillars on the front porch.

"Oh, bring the little dog in, the children won't bother her," I said, thinking she was concerned about her little white poodle being teased by small children, for every child in town loved "Shee-Shee".

"Oh, no, she might pee pee on zee floor," responded Ruby in her delightful French accent.

We went inside, she looked briefly at the three beds left in the house and bought them all. We had a short conversation about the weather and she declined my offer of tea or coffee. I had not thought to offer sherry.

Betty Mackie in the garden of the Black house

That afternoon I did have a tea party for some of my friends and a new woman in town, the wife of the new bank manager.

This lady was diminutive and demure, with impeccable manners. She gave the impression of having led a sheltered life. It was something of a surprise then when the Black house and Ruby's morning purchase were the only topic of conversation.

"You know," I said, "what I can't understand is where she is going to put all those beds. That two-storey frame house she has on Second Avenue has three bedrooms, I am told. And she already has some beds, hasn't she?"

Everyone agreed it was a puzzle, but our prim bank manager's wife had the solution.

"Oh, I think they need them for all the men; and the women themselves just hop from bed to bed, don't they?"

Betty with daughter Laurie in Dawson City circa 1950. The buildings in the background were among the oldest in North America.

Three years after our summer in the Black house, I had the privilege of meeting Martha Black, the first lady of the Yukon on the day that Dawsonites celebrate the discovery of gold. It was August 17, 1955 when she made the trip to Dawson City at the age of 89 and was honoured at a public reception hosted by the Chamber of Commerce while she held court from her wheel chair.

When she returned to her home in Whitehorse we learned that she had been upset at the general state of decay and neglect in the city. "Dawson is a wreck. I saw three of my old homes . . . It just made me heartsick," she was quoted as saying.

She died on October 31,1957 at the age of 91, but she lives in my memory as a most courageous lady, and the summer we spent in her Dawson home is one of the most pleasant memories my children and I have.

———◆———

THE CAMP AT INDIN LAKE

By Hilda (Weichert) McIntyre

I was still a teenager when I went north to Yellowknife in 1943. My first job there was as cook/manager of George Harvey's Squeeze Inn Cafe. The cafe was located in the "Old Town" on Latham Island.

When George Harvey sold the cafe about two years later, I accepted a better paying job off with Paul Glidden. This job was that of camp cook for about a dozen men in Mr. Glidden's exploration camp located on the shores of Indin Lake some 100 or 150 miles north of Yellowknife.

We flew out to the camp in a floatplane piloted by Ernie Boffa, or perhaps it was one of the other bush pilots of that era. The camp was a collection of shack-tents set up on the shore of the lake. The cookhouse was a large tent with the kitchen area at one end and a long plank table, with benches down each side, taking up the remainder of the space. A provisions tent where canned goods and groceries were stored was located a few feet in front of the entrance to the cook shack. My living quarters, which I shared with my little dog Elmer, a miniature Spitz, were a smaller tent attached to the back end of the kitchen.

Hilda and a bush plane

The camp cookhouse

I had to keep an eye on the little dog because the wolves often prowled around the camp and he would become very excited and bark to go out and chase them. He would have made only a mouthful for one of those hungry creatures. On more than one occasion the wolves stole Elmer's feeding dish, even when I tied it to a tree with a piece of string. The only solution was to bring in the dish with the dog after he had his evening meal.

I did all the cooking and serving of meals including baking bread and pies in the oven of a small sheet metal camp stove. The wood supply and the hauling of water from the nearby lake was the job of the "bull cook", a man whose name was Leo Dubois.

It was on one occasion when all the exploration crew, including the bull cook, were working on showings several miles from the camp and I had just baked a batch of bread, that I had an unexpected and unwelcome visitor.

In the provisions tent there were a number of shelves for storing groceries and a couple of empty ones where I could place my fresh baked bread for cooling. On this occasion I had just put out the hot, fragrant loaves to cool and returned to the kitchen to prepare the evening meal when Elmer began barking and making a terrific commotion.

I went to the front of the cook shack to see what was causing the dog so much alarm. Upon opening the door I saw the rear end of a huge black bear protruding out of the open door of the provisions tent. He was happily munching away on one of my freshly baked loaves. Hurriedly shutting the door of the cook shack I dragged the long dining table against the door to bar it from entry by the bear. Then my anger overcame my fear. That bear was eating the bread I had worked so hard to produce!

Grabbing an armful of stove wood from the pile near the stove, I climbed onto the table, opened the canvas flap above the door and began throwing sticks at

Hilda, with George Harvey and his wife, owners of the Squeeze Cafe in Yellowknife, 1945

the bear. He was only a few feet away so I had no difficulty in hitting him. Startled by this attack, the bear forgot the bread for the moment and backed out of the tent. Each time he would start back I would throw another stick of wood and scream at the top of my voice. I had no idea what I would do if he decided to attack my flimsy shelter. The bear appeared confused and tore at the ground in anger sending up showers of dirt. Just when I thought he was about to attack he backed off and slowly made his way slowly into the surrounding bushes. It was then I heard the welcome sound of an outboard motor and the voices of men singing out on the lake as they made their way back to camp.

At first, doubting my story, the crew made fun of me but had to believe me when confronted with the evidence of the broken shelf, torn up ground, bits of bread and scattered pieces of stove wood near the front of the tent.

That spring had been a bad one for bears at a camp across the lake and the foreman at that camp had borrowed Paul Glidden's rifle to deal with a bruin that was making a nuisance of itself around his camp. That left our camp without a rifle.

This is where the experience of the old bushman Mr. Dubois, the bull cook, came to the fore. Expecting that the bear would return to where it had located an easy source of food, Mr. Dubois. made preparations. From the camp's explosives cache he took a few sticks of dynamite, a blasting cap and a short length of fuse. Inserting the cap, with fuse attached, into one of the sticks of dynamite he tied the rest of the bundle around it. He was ready, and we didn't have long to wait.

After finishing the supper dishes that evening I took the dishpan of dirty dishwater and walked over to the brow of the hill where I intended to dispose of it over the bank.

A dog team in training on bare ground outside Weaver & Devore's General Store in Yellowknife in 1944

Just as I prepared to throw the water the bear appeared at the top of the bank. Startled, he rose to his hind legs and I let him have it dishpan and all. Whirling around, I retreated to the safety of the cook shack as fast as my legs would carry me.

The Bull Cook and another man cautiously approached the bruin. Dubois lit the fuse on the bundle of explosives and threw it toward the bear. The bear ambled over and sniffed curiously at the bundle with its sputtering fuse. The resulting explosion sent him rolling over and over down the hill. Upon reaching the bottom the injured bruin, probably blinded and deafened by the shock of the explosion, scrambled to his feet and began to run straight back up the hill to where I stood with the men from the camp.

We took off in all directions. One of the drillers and I, both trying to get into the cook shack at the same time, got stuck in the narrow doorway.

The bear, passing within what seemed to be inches of us, dashed between the tents and into the woods beyond where we could hear him crashing away into the distance. I am happy to report that bear never bothered us again.

———————◆———————

LIVING IN A TENT ON GORDON LAKE

By Kay Muir

I first experienced life North of 60 in the summer of 1937 when my husband Ken and I lived in a tent on the shore of Gordon Lake, which was about a 30 minute ride in a bush plane away from Yellowknife. The property was called Camlaren, named for the prospectors who had staked it, Don Cameron and the McLaren brothers.

It was truly a canvas compound. The 50 or so men, the staff, even the cookhouse were all contained in tents. It was surely a new experience for me as before I married a mining engineer I lived only in big cities.

But it was very exciting - the beginning of the Yellowknife Boom. We were constantly surprised by visitors arriving in very official looking planes - one day it was the Governor General accompanied by a bevy of newspapermen including Pierre Berton and Gordon Sinclair and we all shared lunch in the canvas covered cookhouse.

I had to leave all this excitement and go out to Edmonton before freeze-up as I was pregnant and Dr. Ollie Stanton had not yet come to live in Yellowknife. Our first son, Allan, was born in February and we took him to the little house that had been built at Camlaren while I was away.

Kay washing laundry at Gordon Lake, 1937

Nearly a year later it was decided that the cost of taking machinery and equipment in was too high to make the mine pay so we moved to the Thompson Landmark Mine.

And it was there that I had my first woman friend in the North! Hugh Fraser, the geologist, married and brought his bride in to live in — guess what — a tent!. Betty and I shared a lot of things, including a very temperamental Coleman iron that sputtered fire and scared us half to death. We are still number one friends and carry on a very spirited correspondence.

Much later in 1946 we again lived in the NWT, at Giant Mine, until 1951. Ken died very suddenly soon after we moved back to Toronto. The friends from the early days were, and still are, a very large part of my life, and I am very grateful to have known them.

◆

A LIFE FULL OF HARDSHIP
AND EXCITEMENT

By Mildred O'Callaghan

I was working in Dr. Shillabear's office in Westaskiwin when I decided to go North to Fort Smith and marry my childhood sweetheart Denis O'Callaghan. I knew it was rough, primitive country but I went anyway.

Two years later in 1938 we drifted down the Slave River on a raft of two logs and a few old boards because we had no money to go anyplace else. We met so many men leaving Yellowknife because they could not get work at Con mine, the only mine in the NWT at the time. Neiland and Harcourt were bringing them out as far as Fort Smith on their boat free of charge. It sometimes seemed that we were going the wrong way.

Fred Jacque picked us up on the banks of the river one morning. He had a nice boat and asked us to go to Yellowknife with him and his three sons, Freddie, Hubie and Harvie. Denis had been to Inuvik three times so could help Fred on this trip. They treated us royally. I remember the boys making bread.

We ran into a storm and had trouble getting into a cove but we made it across. Denis loaded a grubstake on our makeshift log raft so we had no problems with food.

Denis and Mildred on their wedding day in Fort Smith, Northwest Territories, 1938

Once set up in Yellowknife I was invited to have coffee at Dorothy Cinnammon's house. Ted's mother was there, Velma Cinnamon. They said there were 17 of us girls here now: Mildred Hall (McMeekan), Joan Vashon (Benkie), Vickie Lapine (McCale), Lill Bretzloff, Elsie Umbach, Flo Racine, Margaret Wylie, Flo Ingram and her sister Chris Campbell, Helen Perkins, Largen, Pearl Clayton, Betty Neusell, Lu Phillamey and Mrs. Thibert.

I don't know if I have this right but I think some women had left when the war started and returned later. Marnie Perkins and Alice Johnson returned. Ruth Stanton was living in Yellowknife I think but maybe at the mine. There were many families living at Con and Negus mines. Most of the people lived in tents to start with. We used orange crates and butter boxes for furniture. Burns and Company Manager Bill McGruther and Johnnie Schurman supplied this furniture.

We met people my husband had befriended at his home in Fort Smith. One gave us his house for the summer and one helped Denis get work at the mine. Henry Glucing gave me the use of his bakery plus flour and everything needed to get started to start a bakery.

I remember going for the mail but sometimes the wicket would be closed while Elsie Umbach would be reading her letter to husband Art while he was sorting other mail. There was lots of activity around the rock where we lived. That's also where the planes came and went from day and night. Miners, all polite and courteous, were coming and going as they worked three shifts. The pilots brought Bear Lake salmon with them and laid them out on the dock for anyone to take.

There were two government buildings across the narrows, one had liquor stored in it. The first beer boat came in that summer and the shore was lined with miners wanting to get work unloading the beer boat for 45 cents an hour. The other building had two employees, Paul Trudell and Lloyd Bonnyman. They recorded mining claims and whatever else government people did in those days. One day I went in to buy a lot to build on but they did not have any. Lloyd told me we could set up a shack next to Weaver and Devore's store as it would be a road allowance, so we did.

Later we moved up to Frame Lake where we were the only ones until the Lemay family moved in at the south end of the lake in 1941. The town was surveyed finally in 1946 by Paulson.

With so much water around there were drownings. Our good friend, Paul Treadgold, a policeman from Fort Smith was on his way to come and live in Yellowknife when the plane he was on unexpectedly landed up in the Yellowknife Rapids. Three guys were struggling in the water, as their canoe had upset. Tom got two out but the Cushner boy was caught in a fish net and both ended up drowning.

The first cemetery had mostly suicides or drowning victims. Others were killed handling explosives in the mine work, many were lost in plane crashes. Bert Neiland of Neiland and Harcourt Transport disappeared on the lake in January. They were bringing a cat trainload of freight to Yellowknife and ran out of fuel so Bert took off by himself to walk to town. A big search was made but they figured that he slipped through an open pressure ridge. Chuck McAvoy disappeared while flying to a mine farther North and there were many other sad incidents.

The Yellowknife Ladies started a club called The Daughters of the Midnight Sun. Mrs. Geigerick had girl guides and Brownies over to her home quite often. July 1, 1941 the first celebration was held at Frame Lake. The Groats started a theatre, which was a great pleasure to all of us; there was something for everyone. There was a theatre built at Con Mine too but when the mine closed during the war the theatre also closed. That's when Yellowknife became like a ghost town.

Denis mushed his dog team across Great Slave Lake in February 1943 and got work at the DEW line in Fort Norman. The mines reopened in 1946 and once again Yellowknife started to grow. Many of the first comers came back.

In the meantime Denis and I had tilled up muskeg and started a ten acre market garden where the loveliest vegetables the world has ever known were grown. It was too big for the area at the time. We started a grocery store across from the Bank of Commerce as well to sell our produce and it was very successful. It was one of the many ventures we tackled.

Johnnie Dennison who hauled freight and built a road further north asked if he would recommend gardening in the north as an enterprise and he replied, 'No, that would be pretty foolish'.

This was a great life full of hardship and excitement but a real challenge for young people at that time. Everyone was independent but always helped one another.

The O'Callaghan house, Yellowknife, 1945

I can't think of one person in the North that I knew that I didn't admire. We made a great family and laid the cornerstones. Together we did it and I doubt if it wasn't for us if there would be anything there. I don't mind tooting my horn at all. I hope I have told and impressed on you all of the courage it took of us, to have the ability to cut your own wood, pack everything you needed in pack sacks for a mile or two, and have the men working underground in pretty primitive conditions in those days and coming home sick from being gassed.

In 1967 after 29 years in the North we moved to Matsqui and bought a 20 acre run down farm where Denis raised Holstein heifers and rebuilt the farm. In 1973 when Denis was getting ill with emphysema we sold that and moved to Summerland. Denis died in 1990.

Every summer there in the Okanagan, Northerners get together in mid-June near Kelowna and it is a real treat to go and meet everyone and remember the old friends and times.

———◆———

SHE NEEDED AN ASSUMED NAME
TO GO NORTH

By Claire Parker

*M*y story commenced in May 1945 (VE Day actually). I was in Edmonton preparing to fly to Yellowknife to visit my sister, Frances Buchan, her husband, Jerry, and their son Viven. I was briefed on the phone about my ticket and to my surprise, a borrowed name, as I was to travel on a pass, owned by one of the other pilot's wives. It was a cold trip. We sat on benches with our feet on cone boxes that filled the aisle.

It was very exciting for me until a man sat down next to me and introduced himself as the boss of the bush pilots and of course knew my 'borrowed' husband well. We chatted about him and his trips most of the way. I remember sitting with my gloves on all the time, partly because of the chill but mostly because of the lack of a wedding ring. It didn't hinder my eating because in those days all the stewardesses had to offer was coffee and frozen Dad's cookies! I assured my seat mate my husband wouldn't be meeting me as he was out flying but probably my neighbor Fran Buchan would be there. We landed on the ice of Back Bay, as the airport was not yet built. Now my adventure really began.

I stayed in Yellowknife until nearly the end of June when I had to return to my home in Calgary and go to work. Many interesting events occurred in that time. During the first few days I met Tom Doornbos with his yoke and pails who asked me if I was a new waitress in town (most single women were), and I also acquired my first liquor permit. Having grown up in a good Presbyterian home my only acquaintance with liquor was one bottle of rum that lasted years and was used only when my father came home chilled from a late curling game. He always went to bed before having his one drink. The bottle remained on a high kitchen shelf and we all knew it was 'for medicinal purposes only'.

In Yellowknife we paid 10 cents for the little boat ride to and from Latham Island where the liquor store was one of two government buildings. We were allowed to purchase one bottle a month. In the boat I received my first proposition, not for my body but for my bottle!

Before I went to Yellowknife my sister ran her own screening process. As my older sister, she and Jerry invited single men to dinner to decide to whom I should be introduced. This makes me sound about sixteen but I was in my early twenties. They gave the gold star to John Parker. He was a new young lawyer in town, long before the arrival of another John, John Havelock Parker who later became the 'Commissioner'.

He told me later he was very surprised to be invited dinner at he Buchans but bachelors were delighted to accept any such invitations to someone's home for dinner. I know it wasn't love at first sight but we were married in April 1946 and have had 50 years together with never a boring experience.

———◆———

THE NORTH'S LEGACY TO ME

By Helen Parker

From my arrival in Yellowknife aboard a Canadian Pacific DC-3 (six hours late!) on a blustery cold night in November 1955 as a bride - to my tearful departure by car in August 1989 as a grandparent of four, life in the N.W.T. is a kaleidoscope of memories. Memories of people and events, of the birth and growing years of two dear children, of joy and sorrow, and of the land - always the land.

Remembering the Yellowknife of the mid 50's - small houses, few stores, board sidewalks, no long distance phones, no highway "outside", no paved streets, but warm, caring people who, partly because of our isolation, forge close friendships that endure today no matter where we live. For me, it was Barbara Bromley and Marjorie Ward whose generous friendship in those first weeks and months meant so much - and still does. They helped this city girl learn about life in a small northern town.

Helen and husband John going boating in Back Bay, Yellowknife, 1956

What fun we had in those early years! There were dances in the basement of the Elk's Hall (the upper part was not completed until 1960) or at the Con or Giant Rec Halls, costumed greetings and farewells at the airport, snow shoeing in winter and picnics in the summer. Many summer days were spent at the beach on Frame Lake, which included lugging unbelievable paraphernalia seemingly required by babies and toddlers. An unforgettable place!

It is, and was, the people of the North that make it such an unforgettable place. People who cared - who shared your joy and sorrow and who were prepared to offer unconditional help when needed. How unbelievably fortunate we were to have been blessed with very special friends through all our years in the North! I can still feel the heartache when the first of those friends left Yellowknife. Yet, others came to fill the void. The wonderful opportunities we had, in later years, to visit the rest of the N.W.T. were unforgettable.

As I think of those trips so many memories crowd in! I think of good friends we made and enjoyed, the visiting and the laughter. I'll never forget community meetings that could go for hours where each person's point of view was listened to with respect and patience.

Music has always been important to me - and so it was in the North. Our early effort in Yellowknife to bring visiting musicians from the South through the Overture Concert Association was a major undertaking. But we enjoyed beautiful music from singers, violinists, a jazz sextet and other excellent musicians. One of the many highlights was a superb concert by duo pianists - who drove to Yellowknife in their Cadillac hauling their two grand pianos in a special trailer! Through concert subscriptions we filled the old public school gym for each concert. There were many hilarious and difficult experiences but our hardy band of volunteers managed somehow, and the final result was worth all our efforts.

Again, across the N.W.T. some of my happiest memories are connected with music. How much we enjoyed the dances in the community halls or school gyms across the North - to toe tapping fiddle music such as played by good friends Frank Cockney of Tuk, Coppermine's Colin Adjun, or Richard Lafferty from Hay River, the wonderful accordion music of the Eastern Arctic. Never to be forgotten are the square dances, jigs, and the round dances where the floor were literally 'jumping'! From the Delta to Baffin Island the dances were often the highlight of the trip. And who can forget the music of the drums? The mesmerizing rhythm of the Dene drummers and the fascination of the Inuit drummers, their stories and songs will always be with me. One of my most haunting memories is of the Dene Drummers playing at Fort Simpson the night

Helen, with her daughter at Long Lake

before the Papal visit in 1987. They concluded the evening with Johnny Landry playing his "Hinana Hoho Hine". The sound of the pulsating rhythm in that beautiful setting and the setting sun is . . . well, whenever I hear that music, it brings tears to my eyes.

And "always the land" - the majesty of the Mackenzie Mountains, the mountains and spectacular fiords of Baffin Island, the sweeping tundra, the magnificent delta of the Mackenzie River, the icebergs off Pond Inlet. One can't fail to be awed by the incredible beauty and every changing terrain that spans the N.W.T.

Around Yellowknife I think of sunsets over Frame Lake, spectacular displays of northern lights, that very special green of the birch trees as they come into leaf in early June and the 'crunch' of snow underfoot on a cold winter's day. Forever ingrained in my memory is the clear blue of Prosperous Lake on a summer's day, the colours of the Precambrian rocks, and the beauty of Great Slave Lake and the Mirage Islands.

No matter how long I am away from the North, I have but to close my eyes to see friends from the North, to hear its music and feel the power of the Arctic. A rich legacy, indeed!

———◆———

MY EXPERIENCE NORTH OF 60

By Gail Pichichero

After a whirl wind romance in Bombay, I arrived in Vancouver on December 15, 1985 and married Mike five days later. The three-week honeymoon went by quickly and I boarded the plane to Yellowknife not knowing what the North had in store for me. I recall these thoughts crossing my mind as I sat through the three-hour flight. "I've left behind my family, friends, an excellent job, wonderful students, to be with Mike, so no matter where I am in Yellowknife or Timbuctoo, I am going to give this my best shot."

Gail's first winter parka

I had seen snow only in picture books, so was I ever excited to see and run my fingers through the glorious white stuff! Night had fallen by the time we reached Yellowknife airport, the tiniest airport I have ever seen. I glanced at some of the people waiting in the lobby. Most were rugged, outdoor types in heavy fur-lined parkas and boots. I looked down at my black high heels and felt incredibly silly.

Vijay, a comic by nature who comes from the city of Baroda in northwest India, greeted us at the airport and led us to his waiting truck. I stepped out the door into -30 degrees C temperature. The Arctic wind sent shivers down my spine and my hands and feet were numb already. This was the first time I knew the meaning of "feeling cold". How should I know what "cold" meant, coming from Bombay where summer temperatures reach a sizzling 35C and where it is jokingly said that there are only three seasons: hot, hotter and hottest.

Anyway, I sat huddled in a corner of the truck looking out the window. The night sky was clear and dotted with stars. There was a bit of a wind blowing and on the road I saw lots and lots of the white stuff - enormous piles flanking the narrow road. How could vehicles ply these ice roads, I wondered. It was hard for me to imagine.

We had barely gone a mile when Vijay's truck packed it in. Just imagine my first night in Yellowknife and here I was stranded in the middle of nowhere. A passing cab came by and took us home to warmth and security.

Next morning, Mike and I walked about the main street, which happened to be about a dozen blocks. I was amazed at how deserted the streets were — just a few cars and ghost-like figures shuffling about in the snow. Oh well, I thought, I can handle this. No more jostling about on crowded streets, hanging off trains packed like sardines, boarding busses that were already bursting at the seams. This was gloriously quiet and deserted.

We've been "out" of Yellowknife a few years now, but I often reminisce about the adventures and misadventures we had in the great Northern outdoors. My most endearing memory is sitting in our old Dodge close to Tin Can Hill admiring nature's spectacular display of Northern Lights. I have never seen anything so beautiful, eerie and magical as those lights sweeping across the night sky, changing, merging, re-emerging in shades of blue, green, white, yellow and pink. I also remember drifting in our canoe on Frame Lake behind Petitot Park after a tiring day working at the day care centre. What better way to unwind and relax.

Mike's ghetto blaster would be playing soft Kitaro music while I would be loose and limpid, gazing at the star-lit sky. Such peace and quiet I had never experienced before. Many a weekend Mike and I would canoe to our 'special island' above Cameron Falls where all we did was read, eat a leisurely meal, listen to music, fish for the fun of it and drift in our canoe. I don't recall hearing another human voice besides ours. This was soli-

Canoeing at Cameron River Falls, near Yellowknife, 1985

tude, tranquility and wilderness in the truest sense. These weekends were so relaxing and rejuvenating that I went back to work a calmer and better person.

I also fondly remember our visits to our friends, Jamie and Brenda's cabin on River Lake. If ever there was a place on earth where time stands still, this is it. Once you are there you have not a care in the world. Those long, lazy summer days when all we did was sit, chat, cook and eat curried chicken and pike, scribble comic drawings in their cabin journal, stroll through some pretty wild bush, canoe on the placid lake and read comic books in the outhouse while Jamie attempted to scare us with growling bear noises. The nights were especially calm when you could hear the haunting call of the loons as you drifted off to sleep, exhausted from doing nothing!

A funny episode crosses my mind, the time when Jamie went to drill through the frozen lake for drinking water. As he almost cut through the ice, he cautioned me sternly to stand well back as the water below would gush out, it being under tremendous pressure! Oh well, the water tasted wonderfully fresh and we all had a good chuckle about my naivete.

The first months, my adjustment period, were not exactly easy. I was in a state of culture shock. I had no job, no family and no friends. I would often walk aimlessly down Main Street feeling cold, lonely and bored. The letters from my students in Bombay saying how much they missed me didn't make it any easier.

But in time I got work as a day care teacher and things began to look up from that point on.

Acquaintances soon became friends and the future suddenly seemed bright.

It has been said cold temperature brings out the best in warm hospitality and friendship. During our three and a half years stay in Yellowknife, we made friends we've come to cherish and with whom we always in touch. After a while of living in Yellowknife, the cold doesn't bother you anymore, because the friends you make bring so much warmth and laughter into your life.

———◆———

THE NORTH HAS BEEN MY 'SILVER LINING'

By Vicki (Cowlishaw) Pilot

I first came up North due to promptings from my mother. I was 25 years old, living in the big city of Toronto, starting on a successful career as a financial consultant with an upcoming consulting firm. Something about turning 25 made me aware and able to voice my doubts about my current lifestyle and how I felt about the 'rat race' of Toronto. I had no goals and had just broken up with my boyfriend of three years because he wouldn't commit to a future with me (he still lived at home with his parents!). I was sitting having drinks celebrating my birthday with a table of my friends and my eldest sister Janet. After hearing me out, my Mum asked, "Why don't you come to Yellowknife?" My first thought was: Why would I do that? She gave a pretty good pitch about Yellowknife and living in the North and it sounded interesting and adventurous. So I decided, "Why not?"

There I was, just three weeks later, much to Janet's surprise, in Yellowknife, even hearing police sirens; I looked out the window of my office in the Yellowknife Housing Corporation. "Oh, there must be a bank robbery," I said to those around me. Laughter filled the air. "There hasn't been a bank robbery here in decades, if ever," they laughed. Well, my big city attitude was definitely naïve here.

A couple of months later, a very tall, dark and handsome fellow walked by my desk. "WOW" I asked a girl nearby, "Who's that?" Yup, you've got it. Bob Pilot Jr. and I started dating soon thereafter and I ended up marrying him about as quickly and impulsively as I moved to the cold North.

After we had been married a year or so I came to know that my husband's dream was to become a policeman. At this I laughed as I could no more see myself as a policeman's wife than of him wearing a gun. Actually he wears the gun quite nicely and I, after 11 years, am a pretty good policeman's wife. After his graduation in Regina, the staffing guys asked Bob if he'd come back up North. By now I was pregnant and had had my fill of the North (for now) and wanted to be with my family of sisters and nieces and nephews who had all moved from Yellowknife to Vancouver Island. So, after spending six years on the island we decided to be adventurous again and went back up north, this time to a small community of 1,200 people in Baker Lake, which is off Hudson's Bay.

Baker Lake was a very interesting place. It was a lot of culture shock for a city girl from Vancouver and Toronto. The first year was very difficult for me to adjust to, staying home with my two little girls, blizzards monthly, not knowing anyone; it was a very trying time. The second year was better as I knew there was another posting coming soon. But we had made some good friends and I had found several things to do. I also got to work a bit. I was hired by the Baker Lake Historical Society to take pictures of a group of elders (there were only 12 of them left) so I enlisted the help of a young man to translate for me and we went off on skidoo to visit the elders. It was very interesting and I was so glad of the opportunity. As an aside, this young man committed suicide last year, I'm sad to say.

I was also able to work at the child care centre in Baker Lake, doing some counseling with young Inuit children who had been abused at home.

Our next posting was Fort Smith. Fort Smith had lots of trees and greenery and reminded me of home in BC. However, work was hard to come by with the affirmative action policy firmly in place by the government. I was disappointed but the positive part of not being able to get work was that I ended up going back to school at the local college and working part time in the women's correctional facility. This was another interesting experience for me to add to my collection of lessons in life. Next we move on to Iqaluit in Nunavut for yet a different adventure.

The last few years have taught me that sometimes there really are silver linings in those clouds.

———◆———

PIONEERING IN THE NORTH

By Ruth Carter Quirke

"Don't change your citizenship," said my husband to be. "I'd like to work in Canada after graduation." So after our marriage in Minneapolis, and the completion of his Doctorate in Geology at the University there, he negotiated a position with the International Nickel Company of Canada, Ltd. We set off for the North and fifteen years of living in the newly established town of Thompson, Manitoba. For me this was a return to home and for my husband, a return to the land where his mother was born and, in a sense for our eighteen-month-old daughter it was a return to her 'roots'.

It was with a real sense of pioneering that we began our life in the North. The town was literally carved out of the muskeg and forest wilderness. Our only access to the 'outside' was via rail some 22 hours to Winnipeg and about 250 miles northeast of Le Pas.

When we arrived we were allocated a small three-bedroom house, which was part of the first community neighborhood. There was a sort of hospital located in two houses just around the corner from our place, three banks that were also in houses and in yet another house, not far down the road was the Hudson Bay store that carried everything from groceries to heavy winter clothing to get us through 8 months of winter. We felt like we had arrived when, a year or so later, a proper hospital was built and the Bay moved into the first shopping centre about the same time.

While our southern friends and family were aghast at our choosing to isolate ourselves, we wouldn't' have traded those years for anything. Of course there were negatives, the hordes of black flies in summer which made outdoor activities miserable at times (we wore beekeeper nets for gardening), the endless dark of winter and the square tires which developed on our cars for the mind-numbing cold during those months; snow in June and sometimes again in August; no competition on food prices; the high cost of living, and the ever present and seemingly bottomless mud in which our children became mired. I used to tape the seams of our daughter's so-called waterproof clothes in order to delay the inevitable mess, which developed inside her outerwear when she played outside during the breakup period.

In spite of these negatives, we settled into our new life, and my husband spent many hours flying in bush planes as well as helicopters over the vast stretches of near tundra and boreal forest in the pursuit of his duties for INCO. In our leisure time, we explored the environs of the town, drove to Moak Lake on the only road available in the surrounding area, and got to know our neighbors, some of whom had been the real pioneers, who lived in camps while the first houses were being built.

During the long winters we never let the cold curtail activities. Schools were never closed due to weather, and our children always walked in spite of temperatures which could sink to -60F. We made our fun by holding picnics outside around fires built in -20F, tobogganing down the nearby snow covered slopes, cut free Christmas trees and skated on the neighborhood outdoor rink. We made any event and excuse for a party and held really sophisticated black tie affairs. Full length gowns were the norm for the ladies, along with 'Thompson slippers' (rubber boots) which enabled us to negotiate the ever-present snow. We all carried our shoes in fancy bags.

The time passed quickly and suddenly, it seemed, we had been in Thompson for several years. We made our first trip out and our daughter was terrified, then fascinated to see horses, cows and other common domestic animals for the first time. Her first city bus ride was a major event in her young life and she would ride for hours with anyone who would take her.

About this time a road was cleared from the town to Paint Lake, located approximately twenty miles away. We acquired an 18' freighter canoe and spent many happy summer days exploring the intriguing bays and islands there, eventually leasing an island from the Crown. Over several summers we built an A-frame cabin on this property. It was a wonderful venture. We used much hard labour as we located, felled and towed 30' trees across the lake behind our canoe to use as beams for the platform and deck on which the cabin was to be built, dug a privy, cooked over open fires, dried diapers over bushes and sleep in a tent on the cabin platform we had just erected. Construction took years because of the short summers and the complicated arrangements to transport materials six miles from the mainland to the island, then hauling it all 30' up to the building site. It was our unique hideaway and we had so many happy summers there.

During our years in Thompson we saw many changes like the development of an airport with twice daily jet service; the completion of a road to Winnipeg through remote inter lake country and Grand Rapids, Manitoba; a library built and the first collection was 300 books collected over the years by the original Ladies Club and, an increase in population from 1,200 to 14,000 by which time we were transferred to the US.

It is amazing in a small community where you have only each other that people can make their own fun and live very full lives far from the distractions and turmoil of so called civilized centres. There were many compensations, the wild life around us was marvelous, watching a wild fox and a neighbor's cat play hide and seek amongst the rocks at the back our house, appreciating the pristine clarity in the air during the warm summer evenings and sparkling ice crystal on a -55 day, the incomparable wonder of the aurora borealis or seeing the sun set and rise again within just a few hours.

We are grateful and feel privileged to have been a part of an adventurous life in Canada's North.

————◆————

ABLE TO COPE WITH TRAUMAS

By Patricia Reimer

As an employee with Northern Affairs and Development, my husband, George Reimer, arrived in Aklavik in late spring and stayed in Clarence Bell's hotel while I remained in Hamilton, Ontario with children Joe and Sue for a couple of months before word that our government apartment was almost ready.

A trans-Canada train trip with a two-year-old and a four-month-old baby was adventurous to say the least. It was exciting to fly into Norman Wells, where I discovered that flights into Aklavik were limited so my stay with the baby was quite difficult. Apparently there was no landing strip there and only mail and essentials were flown in. Near the end of my first week in the North I was promised I would be on the next day's flight. But I could see the plane loading the mail and realized there would in fact, not be enough room for my little family. I ran down, leaving the babies in my room, and had a fit of hysterics in front of poor Stu Hill, the pilot. He promised room for me on the next day's flight and sure enough the next day we arrived in Aklavik to the comforting arms of husband and father and a short stay at Clarence Bell's hotel until our apartment was ready for our occupancy.

A memorable event happened almost a year later, by which time I was quite comfortably settled and enjoying Northern life. We had installed a large drum beside the stove and George had installed a copper pipe in the centre of the fire pot of the oil stove which ran to the drum to heat the water.

Aklavik in those days had no service people to call upon. One did everything for oneself. Over the year, due to an unprofessional bend in the copper pipe, sediment built up, it became too hot and burned through so that one exciting day we had about 20 gallons of oily sooty water pouring out of the stove. The floor had a slight tilt to the outside of the building so it did not take long to run into the offices below. I ordered our toddler Joe to keep one year old Sue out of the mess and shot downstairs to call for help. When I came back upstairs both children were happily splashing in the mess! Needless to say it was cleaned up and after that I heated the water in a pot on top of the stove.

We arrived in Aklavik with a great sense of adventure. We really fit into the life there and if we had not returned to service in the RCAF we might well have planned a life in a northern community. Our friends were close and fun and have remained friends throughout the years.

The midnight sun is something always to remember. One late evening, George and I went for a short walk leaving the children asleep. On our arrival home we found an RCMP officer sitting in our living room. Apparently our son had awakened and, finding us not there, had taken off and was picked up running naked down the boardwalk in front of Pepher's Store — much to the amusement of several gentlemen enjoying the late night sunshine.

Nothing bothered us much in those years. We were young and any problems were resolved without undue trauma (well after my first week awaiting the flight, that is). We had many interesting trips to other communities and came to know some of the native people and transplanted southerners who lived there permanently.

———◆———

WORLD WAR II WAS YOUNG, AND SO WAS I

By Mary (Mabel Nelson) Sadler

In January 1941, my sister Annie came down from Takla Landing, BC, about two hundred miles northwest of Prince George, for emergency treatment in an Edmonton hospital where I was working as a ward helper. She knew she would need care for her two sons and husband Pat (he was the post manager of the Hudson Bay at Takla) when she returned, so she invited me to go north with her. It sounded like an exciting adventure to head far north and take my chances with whatever might be waiting for me. So off we went.

Mary with 'the mailman and his mail bag' in the snow at Takla Landing

In April there was shocking news from Europe. The Germans had invaded Norway! We agonized over the thought of some old friends, the Vestby boys, there and how they would get along. It would be years before we heard. My sister Sally wrote that Martin, her Norwegian husband, had paced the floor and wept when he heard the news. He still had relatives in Norway and his hair turned white soon after that. Our neighbour, Alec, who had been with the British forces throughout Word War I, offered some thoughts that were slightly comforting.

"These big wars go up and down," he insisted. "We'll beat them yet." He was right of course, we would beat them. We had to. Living under the Nazi boot was unthinkable. We knew Hitler would most certainly not be satisfied until he was running the whole world and that was totally unacceptable for us.

The lack of musical instruments in Takla bothered me more than a little. Our only source of music was the radio, and the reception wasn't necessarily always good. I missed the old piano back home. Pat remembered that he had seen an old piano in an empty cabin on the reservation. That sounded exciting and he took me over to see it. I don't know who had owned it, but it turned out to be just as abandoned as the cabin it stood in. The ivory had long since fallen off the keys, and when I tried to press a key I found it was impossible. The whole thing was so plugged with dirt that it would have taken a major overhaul to put it in working order again, and we were far from qualified for that job. We gave up on that idea.

Then Pat wondered if my sister Esther might be interested in selling her accordion, so we wrote and asked her. She had bought it in Great Bear Lake in 1935, but hadn't played it much. Pat's old gramophone was also still back home somewhere, so he thought it might be nice to have it, and he asked her if she would send it along, too.

I got a bit of a job with the local radio and my Morse code course was coming along not too badly. I'd been offered the job on the radio, which would be for a few minutes in the morning and also in the late afternoon. It was easy enough to learn the characters, but reading them when somebody else was sending was the problem. Then I received a letter from my sister Esther that included a clipping from the Edmonton Journal. It was my horoscope, and one sentence still stands out clearly in my mind. "The things you were born to do may be forced upon you." Well! This code thing had certainly been pushed at me, but whether it was what I had been born to do was something else. Time would tell.

Pat also got the idea to teach me how to do the bookkeeping in the store. I spent a couple of days in the back corner of that dingy establishment, which the natives called "The Smoke House", and after two days I was sure I hadn't been born to do that.

Then it was breakup and the mail stopped for a while. Freeze-up and break-up are the loneliest times in the North. There was no mail for weeks, or sometimes months. There

was no way to get 'out' in a hurry either should the need arise. We filled in the time with reading, and our friend Hans' Book of the Month Club membership was a godsend. He lent us books like 'Gone With the Wind", "My Son, My Son," and one I especially enjoyed was the story of a girl who had grown up on a cattle ranch in Hawaii. It was called "Born in Paradise".

Neil, Mary, Annie and Grant with pelts at the Hudson Bay store at Takla Landing, 1940

Gradually the snow went away, and the ice on the lake was giving up too. The ice had an argument with our little dock on its way out, and Pat had to make some repairs. There was another dock over at the store, and it suffered the same fate. But now we could look forward to the mail plane again. Yippee!

Alec left us that spring, for greener pastures. I'm not sure where he went, but he never did come back, not at least while I was there. Before he left though, he gave me some ore samples in a little container, a few tiny gold nuggets, some ore, which contained silver, and even a little platinum! I still have them. Hans also left for a while, to work with another friend, Eric, up at Harrison Creek. The population was thinning out, but there was old Albert, a bit of a drifter sort, who never seemed to do anything. He was usually hanging around at tea time, morning and afternoon, so of course he was invited in.

Now the ground was thawing out, Pat had to get busy and get a tower built on which to stand the wind charger (hereinafter called the Win-charger, the trade name) which would charge the wet cell batteries, which would in turn power the two-way radio. It turned out to be a good solid tower, quite high, and with a small ladder at one corner to climb on. He had to recruit some help as it was too big a job for one. They also had to install a couple of antenna poles on the other side of the yard. We were just about ready.

In my autograph album I have some sketches of the Frypan Mountains and the date on them is May 5th, 1940. I remember that day well. It was a Sunday, a nice warm day, and I sat on the dock and sketched. The ice was gone by then. My sketches show open water, with swimming ducks.

Mary, with sister Annie and her sons, Neil and Grant, all out for a skate. The Hudson Bay residence and the Win-charger tower are in the background.

In May, the Nazis were up to their old tricks again, invading the Netherlands, Belgium and France. Would they never stop?

It was time now to think about getting the garden in. Pat did most of it, as he had quite a bit of free time from the store, and even though he was working in the garden he was handy to the store, if anybody needed him there. The garden produced the usual things - carrots, potatoes, turnips, cabbages, peas, beans etc. Anything that required very much hot weather though, such as corn and squash were not usually grown. There was a wonderful strawberry patch near the house, and in a few weeks we would be stuffing ourselves with those.

Once the snow was gone, the people on the creeks were more mobile. Eric Shaede had a rattley old pickup truck, and there was a road of sorts, which ran all the way from the Omineca River down to Takla Landing, ending up a quarter of a mile south of Aikens. This was called "The Point", or "D'Aginault's Point", if one felt like being specific. A few years before Mr. D'Aginault from New York came here, all set to make a million.

He had a fairly large company, and built a number of cabins, bunkhouses etc. down at the point. He was also responsible for the road up into the hills, which was where he established his mining operation. At one place up there, I heard he had built a flume, which ran for miles around a mountain to divert the water from the creek so that it could be used in his sluice boxes. Evidently he had had to give up, as he had not found enough gold to finance his mining. His road was still quite useful and his old buildings down at the Point still provided shelter for anyone needing a roof over their heads for a while. I am sure the Tom Creek crew had some sort of vehicle too, although I never saw it. Little Pete certainly seemed able to show up quite often.

And as he promised, he came one Saturday to help with the slipcovers. All afternoon, he and Annie fitted and sewed while I presided in the kitchen. We had dinner and they went back to sewing again. At nine o'clock the Mart Kenny show came on the air. Pete was a fan too and a dyed-in-the-wool Vancouverite. I think he forgot he was up in the bush, the same way I always did, and he got in the mood to dance. He dropped what he was doing and put one hand on his tummy, presented himself before me with a low bow and we did a couple of turns around the room. Then it was back to sewing! Little Pete was fun! The sewing project turned out to be a roaring success.

With summer on the way, the scow from Fort St. James came in, loaded down with freight. The scow was run by Dave Hoy and made several trips during the summer. On this particular occasion, it was caught in a rainstorm and everything on board got a good soaking. When Dave tied up at the store's dock and unloaded, we found Esher's accordion and gramophone, all nicely sewn up in burlap, which was soaking wet, but luckily the water had not soaked through the case and the insides were fine.

Music at last! At Harrison Creek, near Takla, June 1940. In the back is Oscar Schayere. From left to right are nephews Grant and Neil, Ann Schaede, sister Annie and Herbie Schaede, Mary (sometimes known as Mabel), George Kellog and Hans Hankeri with 'Teddy'.

Now I had something to make music on, and I spent a lot of time sitting out on the porch just above the dock serenading the great out-of-doors! An accordion seemed rather loud inside the small house, but outside? Well what did it matter? The fish didn't complain! About this time the natives invited us to one of their dances. This was a new experience and one I'll never forget. The men were quite pleasant to dance with, as most of them dressed up in plain dark suits, except for Willie who wore a light gray-blue suit and looked so very dashing! And they all smelled of shaving lotion. It was a night to remember.

A group of surveyors came in that spring to work in the bush around our area. One mail day, Pete happened to come along and he and Annie and I and the boys walked down to the post office together. There in Aiken's store stood a big curly headed fellow beside a pile of gear. He had evidently just come in on the plane and he and Pete immediately got into a conversation when they discovered they were both from Vancouver. The stranger introduced himself as Bruce Lytton and explained that he was a surveyor. Any way you looked at it the scene was getting more interesting.

◆

This is one chapter of a book Mary is preparing about her Northern adventures.

A CHRISTMAS LETTER TO MUM AND DAD

By Mary Saich

It was in 1940 that I experienced my first Christmas in Aklavik. I was one of two teachers at the Anglican residential School. I was young, the only cherished child of my parents and it was my first Christmas away from home. While I was there I wrote long letters home. We had six mail deliveries a year and my parents kept all my letters. I have them before me and my account of that Christmas is taken almost word for word from these letters.

Aklavik, N.W.T.
December 27, 1940

Now listen, my dear Mother and Dad and I shall tell you a story — a true story set away Down North where Santa presides.

'Tis the night before Christmas and at seven o'clock all is ready for the concert. 109 little Eskimaux and Indian children are lined up in the big dining room ready to go on stage. 109 jet-black heads are shining, 49 boys are decked in their scarlet sweaters and nay breeches; 60 girls are standing proudly in their red middies and navy skirts. I wish you could see them.

Anglican residential school staff in Aklavik, 1940. Back row: Grover, C. Searle, Canon Shepherd, Mary and Mr. Rawlings. Front row: M. Punter, H. Sowden, Ms. Miller, Mrs. Shepherd. Photo courtesy of NWT Archives, Yellowknife

'And now they sing "O Canada" and the concert begins. The children really excel themselves and seem to forget their shyness. The Nativity Play is colourful and very well done. The boys do some club swinging and the girls some folk dances. There is little speaking but a lot of singing, which the children do with gusto.

'And now Santa's bells are ringing and in he comes. Each child receives a present and joy abounds. Afterwards we all wend our way to the big dining room for coffee and doughnuts.

'Someone comes running down the hall. Radio messages are coming in. The staff dash upstairs and gather round Mr. Rawling's radio. Miss Nixon beams with joy and tears when her Mother speaks to her from Brandon. Mac, the Hudson Bay Company boy, hears his Mother and Father speak to him. Ms. Shepherd hears her brother. And so the messages travel north. We feel very close to home in that crowded room.

'But our 300 guests, we must return to them. By now the halls are crowded. We meet many of the parents and they all tell us how proud they are of their children.

'Santa has finished giving out his gifts to the staff and gradually the crowded halls are cleared. Now, we gather in the kitchen for tea and Christmas cakes. Finally we go upstairs to our rooms, but the night is not over.

'At 11, we don our mukluks and parkas and woolies and are off to church to the midnight service. Once in our surplices we file in a small choir of six. The pews are packed. Mr. Jones gives us a wonderful sermon on Christmas. Then comes our anthem "All Hail

The girls' Brownie pack on an outing in Aklavik, 1940
Photo courtesy NWT Archives, Yellowknife

To Thee Emanuel". In the second verse the tenor slips in his "All Hail" and we very nearly break up in laughter. However, we do finish with decorum. At 1:20 a.m. we take off our surplices and head back to school and bed.

'I had asked Miss Miller, the girls' supervisor, to wake me before she gets the girls up so at 7 o'clock I am donning my bathrobe. Click, click, click and the lights are switched on. Kerplunk as 55 pairs of bare feet hit the floor. Of course the girls have been awake for ages. Now they rush to the washrooms where their stockings are hanging. Such oh's and ah's. "Oh look, Miss Miller, oh look, Miss Saich. What's this?" Imagine 55 girls opening stockings!

'Then I go to the boys' dormitory at the other end of the building where the scene is repeated. Balloons are popping and "Merry Christmas, Miss Saich" greets me. Pandemonium reigns. Fun! Fun!

'I go back to my room and discover a stocking on my doorknob. In it are such treasures as a face cloth, toothbrush, soap, pen and pencil and woolen stockings.

'At eight o'clock we have breakfast and morning prayers. At 10 o'clock Santa arrives again to unload the children's Christmas tree. There are such lovely toys for them and it is wonderful to see the happy faces.

'After the excitement we go to our rooms to put on our best dresses and to come down and serve the children their Christmas dinner. Nice roast caribou, roast potatoes, turnips, and lots of gravy. I think nearly all of them have a second full helping. Then real Christmas pudding and sauce and again - two helpings. Later we staff gather in the kitchen and have a snack.

'In the afternoon the children play with their toys and I visit in the hospital. At 3:30 we have a carol service for the children in church.

'In the evening we staff have our dinner. We have managed to get a turkey sent in at an astronomical price. The table is decorated with coloured lights and small spruce boughs. There are a few candles lit here and there and when the main light is turned out it is truly beautiful. We have several guests from the village and we enjoy a tra-

Mary and boys from the Anglican residential school in Aklaviik enoying the outdoors during warmer weather in 1940.
Photo courtesy NWT Archives, Yellowknife

ditional dinner, superbly cooked by Miss Searle, our kitchen matron. And talk about magic. Mr. Peacy, the radioman, arrives with a radiogram for me.

'Afterwards we all retire to the sitting room and manage to have a singsong of carols and wartime songs. Mildred and Kitty sing us some songs and I kick off my shoes and do the sword dance over a couple of yardsticks.

'About 11 o'clock our guests leave and we retire to our beds and, not surprisingly, to sleep.'

———◆———

ICE FISHING IN HUDSON BAY WITH THE INUIT

By Sue Shirley

This story will share a single, small event in my 15 years living here on the shores of the West Coast of Hudson Bay. It may begin to answer the question, "Why do you stay up there anyway?" which I have heard from so many southerners.

The town I live in, Rankin Inlet, has about 1,600 residents and is surrounded by seemingly uncountable miles of inexpressibly empty space that reach beyond imagination, to other equally remote lands. It is this space, this limitless tundra that is the attraction to me. It keeps me here, and chances to travel beyond the usual trails are eagerly accepted.

On the three day Thanksgiving weekend of 1992, I joined some Inuit friends on an ice-fishing trip. The fall ice fishing is an event much appreciated, but one that I had never been on so I happily accepted the invitation. I went with Louisa, her husband Sam and his mother, an old and very traditional lady, Mrs. Tiriak, who had been recently widowed. Probably the only reason I was asked is because I'd been bragging to Louisa that I was now a long distance ATV (All Terrain Vehicle) rider and all summer I'd been bouncing over vast reaches of tundra even off the trails on my three-wheel vehicle.

Before embarking on any trip, I often feel nearly sick with a sort of nervous anticipation and so it was with this venture. The day before, my husband Jim, had changed the ATV tire, sorted out gas for my machine, I bought food and located all my out-on-the-land clothes; long johns, wool pants, wind pants, sweaters, down jacket and outer parka. Remember there would be no place to warm up except a tent which was heated by a Coleman stove and that, only at the discretion of the lady of the tent.

I recall other trips where when I popped into a tent I found that people were all merrily fishing, the stove was cold and the little haven of coziness was chilly and unpleasant.

Food being packed and the first layer of clothes on, Jim and I went out to load up the ATV, lashing my sleeping bag, foam pad, a few extra clothes and the edibles on the back rack. No word from Louisa yet, but I wanted to be ready. It was a good day for such an event, wind from the southeast, which would put it at our backs while driving. My biggest worry was my perpetually sore right shoulder - a legacy from earlier bumpy rides across the tundra. But from Louisa's description of our planned route, we would be on lump free newly frozen lakeshores. My aches and pains could relax.

Just then my friends pulled up, their machines loaded and with little old Mrs. Tiriak neatly tucked in behind Louisa and their gear. I dashed indoors, threw on my outer clothes and rushed out to my adventure. Jim would stay behind and work on his project and cook up a Thanksgiving dinner for Monday!

We tore out of town, and already I could feel my shoulder was alarmed at the activity. The road to the turn-off is wide and smooth and our machines raced along at top speed. The rocky land slowed us as we swung to the left and entered the Diane Trail.

The tundra vista and the land are like a rocky beach, the rolling hills like sand dunes, with no trees or other major vertical obstructions. You can drive without really dedicating all of your consciousness to it - once you have some experience the proper approach to the lumps and bumps can be nearly without thought, although there are some areas with more difficult hummocks of peat and grass standing up in hollows of sunken bog. A rough terrain, it doesn't have to be dangerous if you can find the balance between relaxation and alertness.

Gritting my teeth against the jolts as we attacked the trail to the Diane River (a formidable path in summer but, hopefully better now) I felt sure the trip would still have its rough surprises. The frozen land did make it much easier, we skimmed above the murky peat areas in the lowlands, and I laughed at their lost power. In summer these medieval peat bogs gobble up your tires and cause muck-laden delays while the mosquitoes swarm. They deceive and attract the driver into what seems so safe a path, only to reveal their true nature. Now, frozen and lightly dusted with snow, they were the smoothest trail.

Sue dressed for a cold outing on the tundra at Rankin Inlet

Louisa and Sam raced along, clear in their knowledge of the route and destination. I was determined not to lose sight of them, as I felt as attached to their leadership as a child to her parents. Of course, this meant I had to keep up to their speed and as we approached the edges of the first lake - then they split up! Louisa independently skimmed across the inner shore while Sam ranged to the right on a subsidiary ice patch. I determined to stick with Louisa as I felt she would keep track of me a little better, despite the fact that Sam was one of the most astute land-goers in the area.

It seemed as if we were the first passengers the lake had seen this fall. The ice is about 1-1/2 feet thick by now on the edges but the centres are totally unknown and nobody drives too far out unless they are certain. I kept close to Louisa as we drove across the lake. My shoulder was now feeling a strong ache and I struggled to adjust my driving posture to take most of the stress in the left one and I asked myself how totally insane had I become? But the answer was immediate - not at all, nobody had such a great chance. I knew enough to get along and stay warm and the heck with discomfort. I'd taken an aspirin.

The trail continued on. I recognized the area in general but the little snowy pockets had changed the familiar and the scene was almost like new. We drove on and on, over other lakes, separating and reuniting, coming finally to a rise that overlooks the great expanse of frozen plains and tundra below. The vista was perfect. Sam, his Mom and Louisa hopped off and lit their cigarettes. I stamped around and bent my thumb back into shape as they smoked. (ATVs are driven with a thumb accelerator) Below us wending through the path and climbing toward us were three other machines. The group proved to be another old lady being taken out by her younger son and two other teen-age boys. I knew them - especially the boy John. They also dismounted and lit up. Louisa and the old ladies laughed and discussed, Sam and the boys stood a little apart pointing and talking about the best directions to the most fish-filled lakes. I leaned against the machine and enjoyed the sensations of stillness and no responsibility; although part of my con-sciousness continued to point out what a dumb thing it was to undertake such a hard and unknown drive with a sore shoulder.

Departing once more, we bumped down the hill, steering around the largest rocks and riding over the others, our machines proving themselves once again to be amazing vehi-cles. The secret is to stay relaxed, let the machine take the stress and yet guide it wisely as the sometimes jagged and impassable terrain unfolds before you. The frozen lakes began to be yearned-after respites in our long journey. I really had no idea when or where our trip was to end. We finally passed the last place I'd ever driven before and a great sense of adventure filled me. John, his Mom and friends turned left toward their camp, John pointed and said to me "an owl" as a large white bird swooped away. This was one of the few things spoken in English thus far. Sam and Louisa were pressing forward at a good speed and as we crossed the lake edges, I carefully kept to their tracks, blessing the snow that left the tire prints. They were definitely farther ahead now, I couldn't keep as close as I'd like to and I was wondering how far beyond me they would actually get before looking behind them. Never mind, I drove a little faster; hit the rocks a little harder and caught up for a while.

Now I saw a broad expanse ahead and another lurking fear was realized. We would cross the river. The Diane River is a broad and major waterway with little channels, swirling currents and, I expect, a major channel that doesn't like to freeze solid until some-time in January. I became a bit worried but consoled myself with the thought that Sam would hardly lead his wife and mother into a watery end. Arriving at the banks quite far up river, we found Iqaluk, an older and venerable land-goer also examining the shore for the best crossing spot. Sam, his Mom and Iqaluk discussed things over another smoke and then we all hopped on our ATVs again and sped along. "Just don't slow down," Louisa advised me - a fact, which I already knew. The slippery river-ice looked different than the lakes, and I drove as quickly as possible, always keeping exactly in Louisa's and Sam's tracks. Going too fast on the ice you run the risk of spinning around in a few dozen circles, nothing I wanted on the river, so a fine balance was called for. When we reached the other shore it was most welcome. I am sure I afforded much amusement - the relief on my face must have revealed exactly how I felt about this section of the trip!

After roaming around this area for many years, I was finally across the river - and on into unseen territory. There was a nice trail here which made driving a gentle interlude, and a surprising number of little dwellings and summer camps could be seen. We were in caribou country now for sure; I expected to see our trail's end at any moment. However, on we continued, and although the trail went straight ahead, as smooth as ever, we veered away to the right and attacked the worst landscape I'd yet to drive on. The pace increased too, as my guides led us further towards the elusive lake. I would now never be able to find my way home alone that was certain. I'd reached an almost military state of mind about my shoulder, which never stopped aching and was sending warning pains into my upper arm. After 45 minutes we rounded a low rise and there, before us, was a medium size lake - we were there. Louisa and Sam immediately got their ice chipping instrument - a toq - and their ice jigging equipment, which was tied handily to the very top of their load, and ran to a likely spot to begin the fun. In disbelief I asked if we were really at the lake, and welcomed to hear that this truly was where we would set up the tent.

Now I was to see why people loved the fall ice fishing. I'd only been on spring trips and each hole in the ice was drilled through 6-8 feet of frozen lake. They weren't done casually at all because much effort and usually two people were the minimum requirements. Now, however, holes were chipped into the thin surface in a few minutes and each person could indulge their whims as to where the very best spot really was. We'd come to an area that yielded Louisa a gigantic fish last year and she hoped to find another. Before long, we had four holes and everybody was jigging, their backs to the wind. You lie on the ice and peer down the hole as you jig and if fortunate, you can see the fish swimming about. And so it was. Louisa called to me that she could see one. No sooner had I run over to look below than the fish swam right under me and struck her hook! I watched for another few seconds as she pulled it up then leaned away so the creature couldn't get right in my face. One for Louisa. She was destined to catch many more in the next two days while the rest of us would have to be content with a few each.

After another hour of jigging I saw Tiriak, Sam's mom, leaning over the shore-edge, knocking frozen rocks with other, loose ones, eventually freeing some of the rocks needed to erect our small tent. Her bent and tiny frame certainly didn't seem up to this kind of task but, having been out with her before, I knew she was far tougher than she appeared.

Louisa caught a few other fish and decided the hole was exhausted. She and Sam began unpacking their ATVs, unlashing the orange tape, which wrapped everything. The horizon hovered far in the distance; a tone of gray in balance with the other grays and tans of the sunless sky and land. There was almost nothing to be seen except flat neutral blue-gray ice and flat grayish-tan land with highlights of white snow and black and light green moss. The wind was light, the temperature about 30 F.

Once our belongings were unwrapped the small white canvas tent was erected quickly with ease. Our site was a much-used one and many larger stones were already in place on the flat mossy area, which made the job simpler. The stones are the mainstay to tenting where there is no chance to use pegs; they hold the tent's ropes steady from the wind and secure the inner walls so well that the finished dwelling is airtight and a small camp stove heats it perfectly. Sam laid his gun in a handy spot right next to the tent in case we saw any game. We brought in the bedding and set up the little house with our bed at the back, stove on the right, extra gear around the edges. Suddenly we were all starving and opening our boxes of camp-goodies, we started snacking; first on a hunk of frozen meat then, on tinned oysters and crackers, canned meats and pilot biscuits while the kettle boiled. Everybody had created this situation with no effort, no directions and certainly no stress or confusion. Sam, Tiriak and Louisa had done this countless times and a comfortable harmony radiated from every action. The tea was especially delicious because of the lake water, and I made certain to get my first cupful before it became as strong as I knew the others drank it. (In fact, the next day, Tiriak, when served her well-brewed morning cup of tea, opened her little satchel and took out an additional tea bag which she put into the dark brown liquid for a real cup of tea!)

Thus our first day passed. After we ate and drank and lounged in the snug little tent we went out again to fish. I stayed with Tiriak while Sam and Louisa drove along the edges to toq over other holes, finally becoming tiny spots on the far shore. The old lady was prone on the ice, her arm the only motion as she raised and lowered the fishing jig, searching the lake bottom for fishy shapes. I bent down and looked into the depths of my own opening into the ice. Below, the hook and the piece of bait on its barbs leaped up and slipped diagonally down as I lifted and dropped my arm. Was this the motion of a small and inviting fish? The lake bottom was a rich tawny ochre, the rocks on the bottom also brown and ageless reflecting their anonymity, and the water blue-green. Finally, I rose back to a squatting position needing to use the less sore arm. My feet were cool; I stood, then squatted, again and again and again, to force the blood through my limbs.

I love to ice fish. Mindless, yet full of thought, you divest yourself of all care and truly become as neutral and black as the horizon around you while also engaged in a possibly useful activity. Time gently passed until at last I felt a small tug and then a committed weight as a fish bit the hook. I stood and began to pull upward, eager and determined to keep the fish impaled and flip it away from the hole as it neared the top in case it came off the hook. I didn't want to lose this one. Stepping away from the hole to keep the fish safe, I suddenly felt the slippery ice toss me backward and I saw the fish flip up as I fell hard on my back, my head hitting the ice. The gray sky was a balm above me and I really felt like laying quietly for at least a half an hour to recuperate from the fall. Not actually out, I felt as if I were close to a concussion. Then I remembered Tiriak; I rolled over and saw her looking my way. She would be concerned. Her presence was so welcome, I didn't want to worry her so I stood sooner than I'd wanted to, walking over smiling, she peered at me, concerned. Ducking and bobbing her head she tried to ask how I was.

Had I seen stars? (This by wave at the heavens, then circular arm motions as of swirling stars) I reassured her, my Inuktutut capable enough to say - "I'm all right". How can I describe her wrinkled little face, staring straight into mine, wordlessly wishing me well? Smiling, rubbing my head, more smiles. I convinced her I was fine and we went back to fishing, me to take the hook out of my first catch, her to jig with occasional glances my way. I'd fallen because the lake-ice was still bare of snow and dangerously slippery.

Between my fall and our eventual retreat to the tent at darkness, we fished much but caught few. Louisa and Sam created numerous holes, and at first Louisa often caught one right after the hole was chipped out It was a calm, flat experience, repetitive, relax-ing, and very far from what most of North America was doing.

86

Darkness comes early in the fall and by about seven, we were happy to settle down, eat, drink tea and chat. Tiriak told several stories; long tales of exciting events on other trips while Sam and Louisa listened spellbound. As did I - vocabulary wasn't necessary to feel the excitement and peril of the story about an overturned komatik. My fall was also worthy of a few words. Around eleven Louisa insisted on frying up a few of our trout as a final warmth-giving act before we slept. They were most delicious. We finally tucked into our bags - Tiriak, myself, Louisa and Sam all in a row. The stove was hissing away and three candles burned as Louisa put on her portable tape recorder and played her favourite Inuit music. Sam finally turned out the stove, blew out the candles and we slept as the canvas rippled and flapped in the wind.

And the night passed. I was warm, except for my feet, which had somehow found themselves outside the bag. Still, sleeping in such a cool place with a cozy cover in the wholly fresh air is the most rewarding of sleeps. At first light I was in a wonderful state of rest, probably able to sleep for another ten hours when I heard the pumping of little domestic sounds as Sam began our day for us by starting the stove, pouring of water into the kettle and making other little domestic sounds. Tousle-headed, we enjoyed our coffee while still in bed, carefully passing items from one to another while discussing what is was like outside. I marveled at my shoulder, which was nearly pain-free. Apparently a severe jolting was what had been needed and I now looked forward to painless fishing.

After adequate indulgence of numerous cups of coffee and snacks, we dressed in our many layers and stepped out. The day was much like the last. The land, unmoved, opens away in a broad sweep to distances beyond our imagination. Our holes in the lake needed only a cup to scoop out the thin snow-slush on top and we dropped our hooks. Louisa again caught the first fish. Then I had a tug, I pulled up the fish. This one was a surprise, though! A sort of cat-fish/eel found here, not eaten, considered ugly and thrown back. I took out the hook and as Louisa came over we looked at it's strangeness. Long, snake-like, it thrashed about. We pushed it back and watched as it hung on the water's surface for a while, slowly regaining strength, undulating it's long shape into a final leisurely escape.

It was, perhaps, an hour later that we began to pack up to change lakes and more hummock hopping, was ahead of me. We took only a few fishing things, some food, the stove, and Sam took his gun. Off we went to 'Amarouktalik' - (Place Where There's Wolves). It wasn't far, but over the most difficult land...a phenomenon called 'heads' since the earthen hummocks are round and stand up from the land like hundreds and hundreds of heads. We lurched over them, and skimmed around the lake-shore with care as it had several rivers flowing into it which meant there would be areas of open water. We were looking for a medium hill with a small stone cairn.

These Cairns on lake edges denote good fishing areas and are found all over the tundra. Louisa energetically began chipping a hole as soon as we stopped. Sam came over to help soon we had four holes. The fish, small land-locked Char, began to bite Louisa's hook with a will and she pulled up several. Others of us continued to try. We chipped holes all over, until it looked like a veritable golf course. Tiriak hummed and chanted into the water as she peered into her opening. Sam laughed and commented that now she was really having fun. This slight, elderly woman had spent most of the past two days lying on the ice, raising and lowering a fishing line.

Not long after, two ATVs pulling a long trailer arrived. Nauya, his wife Elisabeth and teen-aged son and daughter joined us. They set up a tent on the shore, started their stove and now we had a small haven to warm up in if necessary. They chipped more holes and Louisa's success drove all on to continued jigging. The idea of possible caribou absorbed Sam and Nauya and taking guns, they optimistically drove off.

They had just disappeared from view when suddenly, on a nearby hill, a group of caribou came into sight, silhouetted against the gray sky as they moved along. At first they seemed fairly unafraid, grazing and walking calmly. Then, more wary, they began a slow lope along the hill, skirting our camp and continued across the lake finally climbing a larger hill and disappearing. This land has countless little clumps of caribou roaming around it. They are not at all threatened as a species and, in fact, they are more numerous than in years before. In encounters like this, one cannot help but feel there is rightness in the process. Caribou are plentiful, easy to catch and, it seems willing to be caught. People take them with care, use almost all and what is left on the land like viscera feeds the foxes and wolves.

Eventually, the hunters returned, the carefully butchered meat packed inside it's own skin, tied on their ATV racks. We fished on, and then left to return to our tent - again bumping over the 'heads' and skirting the river outflows. Nauya and Elisabeth's family who had now erected their tent next to ours joined us and we became two little islands of warmth and light in the darkness. The caribou was unloaded and pieces cut up for supper. The fish were piled up in the back of the tent. We were inside, having yet another cup of tea when Sam called us out to see a 'dog'. There, not at all far, skulked a little white Arctic fox. He'd come to dinner. Nauya had left a caribou head on the ground and the carcass to be cut up and the little fox was interested. Who could say what he would eat?

Sam and Louisa jumped on their ATV's and illuminating him with their headlights, chased the creature around the lake trying to discourage him. The fox easily avoided the two humans, it was really more of a sport to keep the animal wary of us. We could have easily shot him when he stood in the glare of the lights. Rather, it seemed that all parties, animal and human, were having fun in the dark, on the new fall ice.

Elisabeth fried caribou, we cooked various foods, made yet another pot of tea and all of us prepared for our second night. Our accordion dance music enlivened the dark and we visited from tent to tent, and then finally crawled into our beds and the second night passed.

The wind blew, the snow fell and when we awoke, the lakes and the land were completely covered by snow. It was Monday, October 12, Thanksgiving. In the night, the fox and his friends had come and finished off the meat on the caribou head and several fish that were behind the tent. Their little tracks were everywhere.

Another pleasant morning, more jigging in our sparsely populated lake, then we began to collect our goods and pack up. Rather than head home as I expected we returned to Amaruktalik where the fishing was good - especially for Louisa. This sent us over those dratted 'heads' a third time.

Somehow, it was easier and we were soon at the same spot. Our group now had many holes and Elisabeth again set up her tent, our haven.

Then another group arrived. It was John, his old mother and the two teen-aged friends we'd seen earlier. They all had tea in the tent, took a keen look at Louisa's fish and went out to chip holes. We now ranged far along the shoreline. The best holes they say are not far from shore so you won' find people fishing in the middle of the lake. After a short while two more groups arrived, an elderly couple and another family with several younger children. Now the lake was absolutely peppered with holes and others began pulling in fish but almost exclusively from one hole. How odd. But who can say what causes this - what mysterious combination of things that makes one hole gush forth fish and others nearby are just empty openings? Louisa had gone far down the shore and in about half an hour, Sam walked back with about 12 fish tucked under his arms. The enlarged group was enjoying Thanksgiving and each other mightily.

I was fishing with little luck when I heard someone calling out that they saw a fish below their hole (the lucky hole) and throwing my line down a near-by opening, I got a hard pull and caught a respectable lake trout, maybe the largest of the day. I killed it and took out the hook with decent dispatch. Elisabeth who, along with myself, had caught the fewest fish admired my catch. I felt rewarded for my many long hours jigging and stamping about keeping my feet warm.

And thus our day drew to its end. Noticing the fading light, I thought of the trip home and wondered when we would start back when I saw that they were nearly all packed up so I forced my fish into the knapsack, put away my hooks and tied all to the front rack. Sam had packed my major gear to the back earlier. The few children in our group suddenly were dressed in their heavy caribou clothing for the trip.

Our group was ready first; I followed Sam closely to the ubiquitous 'heads'. Now that the light was fading, I cared more than ever to keep his trail in close view; I didn't want to miss the little dips and turns that had avoided the river outflows and mysterious thin ice. We did not drive one particle slower than possible all the way home! Being now somewhat warmed up to the trip, I kept up very well, bending and twisting to the fortunes of the terrain. Sam knew the way so well that he didn't need to use the trail until we'd crossed the river. I was close behind him, driving faster and faster, somewhat behind me I could see Louisa's headlight. It wasn't at all dark, but the lights still gave a helpful illumination of the snowy details as we raced along the lake edges. Finally we slowed down and took stock. The lights behind pulled up and I could see that it wasn't Louisa and Tiriak at all, but the teen-aged boys who'd followed Sam in a daring kind of manly, wild ride. I'd kept up to all them!

After almost five minutes Louisa arrived. We were close to crossing the river but I wasn't sure where it was. We were just starting over a small lake when a group of caribou also trotting across it noticed us and stopped to have a look, and then move on. Soon we were across the Diane River.

So without anxiety or knowledge, the river was conquered and now we began a lovely portion of the trip home on a well used trail, with all the land white and the air crisp, our lights a yellow thread attaching us to each other. All fears were gone, aches and pains subsided, there was only the rolling land, the faithful and responsive little machine and a growing feeling of wonder and accomplishment. With the river behind me, on the main trail, I could probably find my way home without a guide. We still had about a hour to go on this section but it was so very simple: we floated along, taking little bumps easily; somehow the land had gotten smoother. Perhaps it was the newly fallen snow. The bending and turning of the ride kept us perfectly warm. Truthfully, I could have stayed at that moment in time and space forever...and when, finally, the lights of Rankin came into view, underlining our trail's end, I saw them with regret. We continued and eventually hit the main road. Individuals again, we didn't speak but drove in the pitch dark into town, passed by many others also coming home after the weekend. I drove by the student residence, past the water tank and the store and turned up the road to my house. Slightly stiff but immeasurably pleased, I went in and was welcomed by the scent of the turkey dinner.

———◆———

A LONG TIME SWEETHEART
BROUGHT ME TO THE NORTH

By Eleanor Theriault

I thought of the North as far removed from the rest of Canada, so remote that we knew almost nothing of northerners. I suppose I never really bothered to find out about the North as I thought it was some place I would probably never see. I had no desire to go to the land of snow and ice with its Eskimo huts, and I thought it would be lacking in beauty and all the familiar amenities of life. When it became evident I would be going to live in the North, I seriously began to read and learn, and I had quite a change of attitude.

I came to the North to marry a long-time sweetheart whom I had met in 1967. I was divorced and had four teenage children when we met. I felt that I was not ready to meet the demands of another marriage along with trying to raise four teenagers in their most challenging years. My northern husband-to-be waited for many years and we were married at a small ceremony in our home in Iqaluit.

Eleanor and Andy on their wedding day at their home in Frobisher Bay, now called Iqaluit.

My first year was one of excitement and learning, mostly learning.

One was that one never wears high-heeled shoes to walk on the gravel roads unless you are willing to stop and kick gravel out of your shoes every five feet! Another was learning how much to order from Sealift. I've learned by error that a case of mustard will do at least seven years!

At first I missed my old friends in the South, my family and the type of socializing that we enjoyed. I missed the opportunities of attending live plays, recent films and some nice restaurants. But after a while, these places seemed so unimportant. They were special treats for entertainment when we went on vacation in the South.

I missed being able to buy certain grocery items. However, Arctic Ventures, the store where we shopped in Iqaluit in the early '70s, had an unusual stock of items surprising to see in the Arctic (i.e. papaya juice and refried beans). It was so much fun to browse through the store. It has been sold and modernized and has lost some of its charm, but it is still a nice store.

We could phone and have someone in the South shop for us or, while "out" on vacation, we would stock up on items that we had found hard to get. I remember once, a well-meaning girlfriend sent me this huge box of teas, coffee and jams. She was concerned that these items were unavailable in the North; actually those particular items were easy to find. We would buy new clothes when we were out on vacation because the choice in Iqaluit was not great at the time. I also remember once when the Legislative Assembly was held in Iqaluit in the '80s, one lady was accompanying her husband, (they were from Hay River) to the Assembly, but enroute from a visit in Victoria, BC, she had purchased a dress in a Victoria boutique only to find the same dress at 'The Bay' in Iqaluit for a much lower price. One finds you do not put as much emphasis on style as you once thought important such as wearing blue jeans to church or parties.

What I found exciting was not one thing but many things. The whole experience has been exciting: watching the town double in size since I arrived; meeting so many politicians, movie actors, artists and scientists; being included in many social events that made it possible to meet these people that we would never have had the opportunity to meet in the South. We entertained many of these people in our home. Some of the most interesting were the Russians that came to the Arctic. One group was the young and brave lads who did the 'Walk to the North Pole'. We learned about their life in Russia and found that although they differed from us in some ways, their hopes and dreams for the future were the same as ours.

Excitement was being there when my husband was elected mayor of the town; being there when my grandchildren were born; and watching our town on national TV for various reasons. One occasion was when my husband and some of the RCMP arranged to have two horses shipped by air to Iqaluit for the 1st of July celebration. It was the first time in history that a real live horse set foot on Baffin Island. The occasion caused quite a stir.

Excitement is watching a full blown blizzard from the warmth and comfort of your home after you have checked to ensure your family is safe and cozy at home; watching the Northern Lights in winter and enjoying the beauty of the cold winter days and nights with the full moon and stars out, giving the impression that if you reached out, you could almost touch them; watching for April and the return of the Snow Buntings, the most darling little birds.

How much I would have missed not to experience the ships arriving in late August with Sealift. The ships in the bay all lit up are a magnificent sight. I suppose my one biggest complaint is, not the harsh winter months, but the length of the winter.

I loved the challenges that we had to meet and conquer, and the feeling of achievement. The many ways people find to have fun and entertain themselves. I remember with great joy an "Edwardian Party" my husband and I attended once on the first day of summer. It was supposed to have been held on June 21, but it was raining and so cold that we had to have it a day later.

Everyone had to wear a costume of that era. It was wonderful to see what imaginations people have and what they can put together with things they have in their own

92

homes. The party was held at Apex, a small hamlet three miles from Iqaluit. There was a wonderful bonfire blazing and we certainly appreciated the warmth of the fire. Set out on the tundra were tables with white damask tablecloths, silver tea services, crystal punch bowls, cucumber sandwiches, chocolate dipped strawberries and pound cake. A real live string quartet played the music. They were the ones who most appreciated the fire. We played croquet on the Tundra, granted with some difficulty! The washroom facilities consisted of a pup tent with a 'honey bucket'. That was a situation that might have made people from the Edwardian era faint, to see the ladies in their long skirts and petticoats making their way to our version of a 'powder room'.   I could almost hear the gasps of horror of the Edwardian dainty ladies on encountering such uncivilized facilities. But it added a touch of reality and we thought it fun.

In those days the airlines used to offer a trip to see the 'Land of the Midnight Sun'. The flights left Toronto in early evening and arrived in Iqaluit about midnight. Buses would meet the passengers at the airport and take them on a tour of our town. On this evening of the Edwardian party we were amused to see a busload of tourists watching us from the road. I am sure they were wondering if we all hadn't lost our senses.

Iqaluit, formerly known as Frobisher Bay, with the domed Anglican church near the foreground

I remember that party with particular joy, probably because so much imagination went into the thought and preparation.

As a wife, I always tried to be prepared at a moment's notice to entertain people from the settlements, Yellowknife and the South. So many passed through Iqaluit on their way somewhere else. Often people would stop by our home for dinner. It was great to see a new face and enjoy their conversation. I also enjoyed getting used to my new marriage and sharing a new lifestyle with my husband, as well as planning for the future.

As a mother, I worried about my grown children in the South, wondering if they needed my help, wanting to let go but worrying just the same. I found leaving them behind difficult and wanted to phone them every day to make sure they were eating properly and dressing warmly. They reassured me they could manage just fine 'thank you', but I sometimes got a bit panicky if I was unable to reach them by phone at times. I would tell myself I was being silly and overprotective but didn't really accept that. Finally, at two different times, two of my daughters came to visit. They fell in love with this part of the world, found work, moved here, fell in love, got married and their children were born here.

Some of the most outrageous experiences when I first came to the North were the noise the ravens made when they walked on the roof the house. My first night I thought

93

someone wearing combat boots was on the roof. Another oddity was 'the honey bucket' and the somewhat horrifying stories of mishaps that had occurred about them. Then there was the smell of the sewage truck on a cold winter day. I remember one time, my husband's boss was arriving from Yellowknife and I was more than a little apprehensive about his arrival. My husband and I were having lunch when the sewage truck came to remove the sewage. Suddenly this horrible stench and gurgling sound snapped us into action. The driver of the truck was obviously not paying attention and instead of turning the lever to vacuum out the sewage, he turned the lever to blow the sewage into our house! What a mess. Luckily we were at home at the time or the damage would have been indescribable. The smell throughout the house was something that I never want to experience again. We got the mess cleaned up and the house scrubbed with disinfectant and considering the accident, we had it back to a decent respectability when the 'Boss' arrived. I love to tell this story to some of my Southern friends. They are of course, horrified and claim that they could never put up with these problems - the very same attitude I had many years ago before I ever considered living in the North.

If I had not had the opportunity to live in the North, I would have missed the most exciting years of my life. I would have missed seeing my grandchildren grow up here; learning first hand the Inuktutut language and the ways of the Inuit; watching with pride as they started school and hear them sing 'O Canada' in three languages - English, Inuktutut and French; seeing my granddaughters wearing 'Mother Hubbard's' (a pullover parka) which I learned to sew for them. Back in Ottawa I would probably have breezed through my middle years quite content and, in retrospect, perhaps a very mundane life-style.

In the North we are exposed to many challenges along with sad and happy times. We get to know many people from all the settlements, which are hundreds of miles apart. Upon hearing a name you find yourself saying "Oh, yes, that is a Grise Fiord name" and so on with other communities. We get direct exposure to everything from politics, social problems, growing pains and planning. To paraphrase the words of Pierre Trudeau, 'Life in the North is like sleeping with an elephant, one cannot help being affected by every grunt and groan.'

I would never have experienced the warmth of the people here or the friendship. I might have lived my whole life in my comfortable little cocoon in the south thinking that the Arctic had very little to offer; thinking that it was a cold and dark place - a place where the people lived in huts or Igloos, ate raw fish and meat and dressed in skins. I would have missed the beauty that cannot be surpassed anywhere.

What I found most rewarding was my feeling of being part of the North and being accepted by the people living here: greeting the elders at the church in their language, Inuktutut, however poor my pronunciation, and having them return my greeting; being in the delivery room when my grandchildren were born; seeing them grow to respect the native people and become friends with them and learn their language and ways; having friends and relatives visit from the South and feeling a great sense of pride showing them our "Northern Home" and lifestyle; hearing them say "You are so lucky to live here"; having my father introduce me to his friends in the South and telling them, "This is my daughter who lives in the Arctic" and being so proud to do so; the interest people show and the questions they ask and I am able to answer; hearing them exclaim surprise at the modern facilities we have and when they learn we really do not miss very much by living in the Arctic.

And a few more memories are; watching and waiting for Sealift time and the excitement of unpacking our food boxes; realizing that some of the purchases were panic buying and not really necessary; enjoying the fun at Christmas - everyone in town really celebrates the festive season to the fullest; the native games that take place from Christmas to New Years; shopping at 'The Bay' at Christmas Mid Night Madness when everyone must dress in night attire. What fun it is to see the imagination of the shoppers for this occasion; the camaraderie between the shoppers is so much fun; trudging home in the wee hours with what we thought were 'real bargains'; finally seeing a safe home for spousal victims open and

The sight of the Sealift is cause for excitement, as long-awaited supplies arrive in communities across the arctic.

helping with the fund-raising; feeding the birds in spring, seeing them waiting for me to arrive from work and welcoming me by flying around and around my car until I got out to feed them; seeing the flowers bloom in all their splendor and taking pictures to send down to family and friends in the South to prove that we really do have summer and lovely flowers, seeing a herd of caribou in all their grace and beauty grazing on a hillside.

There is also sadness here. Saying goodbye so often to friends who come and go. I cannot remember all the people who have left since I came to the north. The hardest experience of sadness I remember was when a friend and her baby were murdered and then the suicide of the husband. This was an especially sad time for us. There was no answer for such action and no chance to say goodbye. The are drug and alcohol problems, which are not limited to the north, but somehow we feel them more strongly being in such a small community; and of course there is the spousal and child abuse.

The most remarkable person I ever met was, of course, Leah Nutaraq who lived to the age of 107 years. She died in February 1993. Her life and history were so interesting. I remember listening to her once, through an interpreter, as she told of her life as a child. Her father was a white whaler and very fierce. She claimed she was scared of him. She grew up in a place called 'Blacklead Island'. Her dearest wish was to return there before she died and through the efforts of my husband and Dennis Patterson, our MLA then, this became a reality. They arranged for her to travel with the Canadian Coast Guard back to "Backlead Island".

Accompanied by a nurse and an interpreter she arrived at her destination. Her delight in being there was expressed as she stepped down from the dinghy onto the land and exclaimed, "Wow, wow". She then traveled to Pangnirtung where she had spent many years. She was welcomed there by many people who threw a big party for her. Leah danced and laughed until the morning light. Can you imagine the changes she must have seen in her 107 years? From being born in an Igloo to modern life with electricity, TV, cars, bathroom, stores and so on. I remember seeing Leah dance the Highland fling once at a senior's party. She had the stamina of a teenager and the grace and agility that put the best of us to shame. She loved life and was very comical. One time at one of our July 1st celebrations, she was given a small Canadian flag; she stuck it in her braided hair and giggled with delight when she caught her reflection in the mirror. She walked to church every Sunday until the last year of her life. A very brave and wonderful lady.

That was 'my' North, and how I loved it.

———◆———

PETS WERE A NO-NO
IN NORMAN WELLS, BUT . . .

By Marg Wallace

In summer 1957 my husband was transferred to Norman Wells, N.W.T. for a one-year assignment with Imperial Oil. We had been living in Devon, Alberta, a small oil town.

We were to take little other than our personal items, as we would be living in company housing which was equipped with furniture, dishes and linens. We packed up our most precious possessions; our twin cocker spaniel dogs named Topsy and Turvy, and flew by company plane to our new home.

The dogs' appearance at the Norman Wells airstrip shocked the area manager meeting us. We were totally unaware that housedogs were a 'no-no' as they would make a tasty treat for the huskies that roamed in town.

So my husband's first job was to build a completely enclosed dog run and pen, which went from our front door to the side of the house. Otherwise the dogs could not stay.

I was expecting our first child. Due to birthing complications experienced by another town lady, the rule was that expectant mothers had to leave three months before their due date and not return until the baby was one month old. So my husband 'held the fort' and I returned to Calgary in mid-September.

The home in Norman Wells, complete with an enclosed dog run to keep the cocker spaniels safe from local huskies.

Our daughter Laurie Ann was born December 20 and she and I returned in mid-January to the North.

It was not difficult for a new baby to turn day into night and vice versa as at that time of the year we didn't even bother to raise the blinds in the daytime due to the sparse amount of daylight.

We awaited the spring break-up of the Mackenzie River with eager anticipation because a new supply of meat and vegetables would arrive by ship.

By springtime the frozen meats, which had come in before freeze-up, were getting freezer burn and also the selection was poor. Powdered milk called KLIM was used by everyone as was margarine as no dairy products were available.

My days up there were spent looking after our new daughter, taking her out in the sleigh even on the coldest days. Soon winter had passed, the river opened up and the days became longer, so long in fact that in July and August one could read a newspaper outside at 2 a.m.

In the summer of '58 we returned to Alberta where we took up residence in Redwater.

I look back on my year in the North and realize what a wonderful experience it was. Yes, there were black flies, mosquitoes and cold, dark winter days but the very special people that lived there remain in my thoughts to this day.

Marg Wallace out walking daughter Laurie in her northern baby buggy, a wooden box on runners, in 1957.

A TRIP ON THE BIG MAC

By Janet (Cowlishaw) Whitley

For most people, hearing the words Big Mac means only one thing — a date with a fast food hamburger. For me, it is quite different; these words bring spectacular memories rushing forward. For I am one of the intrepid few who dared the Mighty Mackenzie River and thrilled to its adventure.

It all began in 1984 with my mother begging me to come and visit her in Yellowknife. Being born and raised a city girl and a world traveler since the age of 17, I had had no interest in what I thought would be a backwater, mosquito-ridden environment.

But when she told me she was organizing a trip from Fort Providence, at the mouth of the Mackenzie River, down river to Inuvik, well, now she had my attention. This sounded like a real adventure. Added to that, she told me my childhood hero, her brother, my Uncle Jon, was going, too, so that cinched it. Now I was completely sold on a visit to the Northwest Territories.

I landed at Yellowknife airport, well on the runway anyway (they had a small building but no arrival/departure bays) in early July. Since most details had been taken care of we spent a couple of days getting a couple of flats of beer, smoked oysters and caviar so we could toast crossing the Arctic Circle and of course we needed fishing licenses. I had my tour of Yellowknife in the course of these errands, it only took about an hour.

We had planned to have two weeks on the river and then it started to rain. This in a city where all I had ever heard from my mother was, "Oh, it is so nice; never rains in Yellowknife." Well, it sure did this week, and it lasted for a couple of days. Our boats were loaded and we were ready and still it rained, not a good way to start out in two 18' aluminum Lund boats with no tops! It rained and we waited.

Finally a less damp day dawned and off we set for Fort Providence, our launching site 200 miles south.

Jim, Janet, Toni & Jon explore the Big Mac

We towed one boat with our truck and friends Sandy Holmes and Ed Duggan, towed the other boat. I don't remember much of the drive; I slept most of it after trying to find something more interesting than kilometre after kilometre of five-foot-high trees, lots of yarrow and numerous sloughs flash by. We arrived at Fort Providence in mid afternoon, launched the two boats and were away on the river a short time after 6 p.m. The skies had finally cleared and it was going to be a wonderful sunset. Several hours ahead of us we had Lake Mills to get through, we had been warned that if the wind came up while we were on this lake it could be very unpleasant as it is encircled by reeds and there was no place we could have pulled ashore. Given this break in the bad weather of the last few days we decided to go for it. Turned out both the weather and the lake were exquisite, calm and peaceful, we had hours ahead of us and a beautiful sunset that lasted it seemed for hours. It was a bright raspberry colour, I guess the atmosphere is much cleaner in the north because I always noticed the sky was bluer and the sunsets brighter.

Finally around 3 a.m. when we had cleared Mills Lake we spotted an abandoned rock mine with considerable level ground so we stopped to get some sleep. This setting up (and taking down) seemed to me like a ritual from hell. Unload the boat, clear the tent area, find and nail the spikes into the ground (luckily it wasn't all rock!) put up the tent, roll out the foamies and lay out the sleeping bags. Then start dinner and through all of this my Uncle Jon, looking at me out of the corner of his eye, would chortle, "Are we having fun yet?" No, I wasn't, I did not like this part of the trip.

Supper, very welcome at the end of a long day on the river

Then we ate; it became one of the most unexpectedly joyous events. The smell of the morning coffee was heavenly. Foods that I would normally have pitched out if they even managed to sneak onto my shelves in my Toronto apartment were suddenly gastronomic wonders. Tinned smoked oysters, dried eggs, bannock, canned bacon, just remembering them now sets my taste buds tingling. And I could not eat enough!

After the meal, we washed and dried the dishes and pans, I washed my hair and then we repacked the food boxes, we did not want to tempt any animals. As on many nights to follow we'd sit and talk about various aspects of the trip so far, what was coming up next and often, as we had a rifle in each boat, in the evenings we would get off a few rounds, for me it was a learning experience since I had never fired any kind of gun or rifle. It was hard to feel tired and realize it might be bedtime because it never got dark and of course the further north we went the lighter it got. One night when I was thinking it was about 9 pm I looked at my watch and saw it was actually 3 am!

We arose early, did the breakfast thing and then launched out for another down river day. Now in one boat were Uncle Jon and myself and I was the navigator or 'nav' for short. In the other boat were my mum and her friend Jim. Since ours was the lead boat

I was responsible for spotting the rams, they are large triangular shaped pieces of wood with a big line running down the centre of it. When you are correctly positioned on the river there are two rams, one of which you are heading towards and the other which should be directly opposite it behind you. This keeps you centered and avoiding rocks and sand bars. Basically you end up sort of zig zagging down the river as the rams are on opposite shores and you are constantly turning to find the next set. It feels a little dicey if one ram may have fallen down and you lose your bearings.

It seemed we drank a lot of beer and yet I seemed to feel no effect, more like having water. Maybe it's the pollution free air! We had some strange drink combinations that would normally have curled my hair. When we crossed the Arctic Circle we stopped for a toast of gin and Tang! It was one of the most delicious drinks I ever had. I'd have to pinch my nose now to down one, but then it was delicious.

We stopped at several Indian villages along the river. Sometimes many people would come down the river bank to see us, it seemed a bit nerve wracking to me, were they wondering if we were coming in peace or what? The villagers were shy but friendly. In the village store we bought a few cans of items we had run out of. Most of the villages were 'dry', no alcohol, but we did get some from a friend of Jim's in Norman Wells, where it was Sunday and the liquor store was closed.

A wild animal print, not fresh, fortunately!

We stopped at the juncture of great Bear River and the Mackenzie where I decided I would fish and try panning for gold. The fishing produced only rockfish, which must have had teeth judging by the number of hooks I lost so, no fresh fish on this trip. And the gold panning, well the river was freezing cold which led to soul-numbing gold panning, no results there either.

We came across an abandoned mine and spent a couple of hours exploring it. I was fascinated trying to imagine the day-to-day life of the miners who had once lived there and imagining their digging in the perma-frost ground. Getting supplies there must have been a horror and, I wondered, what did they do when they got on each other's nerves.

The second to last day of the trip we still had many many miles to go to catch our flight from Inuvik back to Yellowknife. It was going to be nip and tuck to make it. There it truly was light all night. I completely lost track of afternoon and night, it was really just one long night. We decided over breakfast to ride all day and night to Inuvik so I was happy to help roll up tent and bedding for the last time.

Uncle Jon and I were in the lead boat most of the day. We saw some of the most beautiful scenery and places to pull over to for meals or a break. The air actually sparkled, there was a soft blue sky and the unending sunset was lovely pinks and oranges. We turned into the channel that would take us all the way into Inuvik; overhead there arose a flock of gorgeous white Canada geese disturbed of course by the motors. We wound through the channel this way and that; all was lush green around us.

This last part of the trip took us 17 hours and almost all the way I heard trains! I heard the wheels turning, the whistle blow and looked everywhere for evidence of a train. But, of course, no train. A hallucination I guess.

Uncle Jon told us after we arrived in Inuvik that he had the sensation we were going down hill and his foot was searching instinctively for the break on the floor of the boat! It seemed as though the isolation with only rams, buoys, unlikely food and drinks that we were losing our minds! But what a place to lose them.

We had a hotel room that night with real beds and a hot bath, in a tub, and a restaurant meal and real drinks! Now I am back to my city life in Toronto but with an exquisite adventure in Canada's North to last me through life.

———◆———

ISBN 1552124495-5